DIVINE
SPIRITUAL
LAWS

DIVINE
SPIRITUAL
LAWS

CHANTAL R. NIELSEN

CREATION
HOUSE

DIVINE SPIRITUAL LAWS by Chantal R. Nielsen
Published by Creation House
A Charisma Media Company
600 Rinehart Road
Lake Mary, Florida 32746
www.charismamedia.com

This book or parts thereof may not be reproduced in any form, stored in a retrieval system, or transmitted in any form by any means—electronic, mechanical, photocopy, recording, or otherwise—without prior written permission of the publisher, except as provided by United States of America copyright law.

Scripture quotations are from the New King James Version of the Bible. Copyright © 1979, 1980, 1982 by Thomas Nelson, Inc., publishers. Used by permission.

Design Director: Bill Johnson
Cover design by Nathan Morgan

Copyright © 2011 by Chantal R. Nielsen
All rights reserved

Visit the author's website: www.chantalrnielsen.co.za

Library of Congress Cataloging-in-Publication Data: 2011942168
International Standard Book Number: 978-1-61638-746-4
E-book International Standard Book Number: 978-1-61638-747-1

While the author has made every effort to provide accurate telephone numbers and Internet addresses at the time of publication, neither the publisher nor the author assumes any responsibility for errors or for changes that occur after publication.

First edition

11 12 13 14 15 — 987654321
Printed in the United States of America

DEDICATION

I dedicate this book to my loving husband Bronson who is my soul mate and constant reminder of God's unconditional love toward us. To my daughter Nikita for all her support and encouragement during the writing process. Thank-you my son Jesse for being obedient to the Lord and for hounding me when I wanted to quit and Scarlett my baby girl for your endearing ways and constant interest in the progress of this book. Thank-you Lord for Your Son Jesus who is my life and hope and constant peace in this crazy world we live in.

CONTENTS

1. What are Divine Spiritual Laws? 1

2. Covenant Relationships 15

3. The Birth of the Early Church 25

4. *The First Commandment:*
   You shall have no other God's before Me 33

5. *The Second Commandment:*
   You shall not make for yourself a carved image 41

6. *The Third Commandment:*
   You shall not take the name of the Lord your God in vain. . . 49

7. *The Fourth Commandment:*
   Remember the Sabbath day, to keep it holy 57

8. *The Fifth Commandment:*
   Honor your father and your mother 63

9. *The Sixth Commandment:*
   You shall not murder 69

10. *The Seventh Commandment:*
    You shall not commit adultery 75

11. *The Eighth Commandment:*
    You shall not steal 85

12. *The Ninth Commandment:*
    You shall not bear false witness against
    your neighbor 93

13. *The Tenth Commandment:*
    You shall not covet 99

14. The Bride of Christ 105

   About the Author 117

   Contact the Author 119

Chapter 1

WHAT ARE DIVINE SPIRITUAL LAWS?

Do not think that I came to destroy the Law or the Prophets. I did not come to destroy but to fulfil. For assuredly, I say to you, till heaven and earth pass away, one jot or one tittle will by no means pass from the law till all is fulfilled.

—MATTHEW 5:17–18

DIVINE SPIRITUAL LAWS

THERE ARE LAWS by which nature is governed and there are laws by which the spiritual realm is governed. Newton's Third Law of Motion states "to every action there is always an equal and opposite reaction." This law of motion is just one of the many laws by which nature is governed. In the spiritual realm, every prayer and petition (action) we bring before the Father propels the spiritual realm into motion (reaction). God's angels are propelled into motion when we pray the Fathers will into a situation (positive action) and the demonic realm is propelled into the opposite motion (negative action) by Satan to delay God's will. (In Daniel 10:13, the prince of the kingdom of Persia, withstood Daniel's answer to his prayer for twenty-one days in the spiritual realm.) Every decision or choice you make today will affect the course of your life tomorrow either in a positive or negative manner depending on what laws you have based your decision on. Were your choices and decisions based on the Word and principles of God or were they based and founded on mankind's worldly wisdom? As Christians we are constantly waging war in the spiritual realm against an invisible enemy, this enemy is not made of flesh and blood, this enemy of God and man is Satan.

Ephesians 6:12 says, "For we do not wrestle against flesh and blood, but against principalities, against powers, against the rulers of the darkness of this age, against spiritual hosts of wickedness in the heavenly places."

In order to defeat this enemy we need to be equipped for

What are Divine Spiritual Laws?

battle, a battle that takes place in the spiritual realm. The decisions and choices we make every day with regards to our lives will either have a positive or negative long term effect depending on what we base our decisions on. Are you using the world and its manmade systems as your guideline or are your decisions and choices inspired by the Word of God and His Commandments? These "Divine Spiritual Laws" are divine laws given to man by God Himself to ensure that mankind is equipped to lead a prosperous life with the ability to defeat the onslaught of the enemy, these "Divine Spiritual laws" are the Ten Commandments. God gave the Ten Commandments to Moses on Mount Sinai for His chosen people the Israelites to obey. In order to live a prosperous and blessed life today, we need to apply these Ten Commandments to our lives as Christian's. The Ten Commandments are our guideline for true spiritual living in a world where immorality and unrighteousness are abounding at a rapid rate. When our choices and decisions are based on the Word of God we leave no place for the enemy to misdirect our lives. In Matthew 5:17, Jesus says that He came to fulfill the Law and the prophecies in the Old Testament, prophecies concerning His birth of a virgin woman and His death on a cross. Jesus' life here on earth gave mankind the true interpretation of the Laws moral precepts.

The word *divine* can be explained as, 'of God or coming from God.' The word 'Spiritual' is directed toward the 'Holy Spirit' and the 'Laws' are a set of rules given by God for humanity to obey. In the context of this book, the Laws are the Ten Commandments: divine rules that God laid out for the Israelites to obey in the Book of Exodus chapter 20. These Laws were given to Moses on Mount Sinai by God Himself for the nation of Israel to set them apart from the pagan tribes and nations of that time. God had made a covenant with Abraham

3

DIVINE SPIRITUAL LAWS

and this covenant relationship birthed the Nation of Israel whom God chose as His people. These sacred or holy commandments were not given to the Israelites to punish them or control them, they were given by God as a guideline to bless and prosper those who obeyed them. These divine spiritual laws are moral and ethical laws by which Christians, who are followers of Christ, should lead their lives today in order to reap the benefits of a life filled with God's blessings, prosperity and abundance. When we choose to live our lives laid out by the Ten Commandments we leave no door open for the enemy to enter in and take control. God and His laws will govern our lives, our businesses, our marriages our children's lives and eventually our nation.

> This book of the Law shall not depart from your mouth, but you shall meditate in it day and night, that you may observe to do according to all that is written in it. For then you will make your way prosperous, and then you will have good success.
> —JOSHUA 1:8

This book of the Law that God is talking about is the Torah. The Torah is the Hebrew Bible and consists of the first five books of the Bible, starting with the Book of Genesis through to Deuteronomy. These first five books of the Bible were written by Moses. The Torah refers to the principles of laws and ethics which were laid out by God for the Israelites to obey. Biblical Law in Christianity refers to the Torah as the Mosaic Law, God's Law or Divine Law. The Mosaic Law or Torah refers to a covenant between Yahweh (God) and the Israelites. In Joshua 1:8, the Bible teaches the key to making your way prosperous and having good success, is to meditate on the Word of God, day and night. When we live a life meditating on God's word which is alive, our lives begin

4

What are Divine Spiritual Laws?

to transform. We begin to attract God's blessings, prosperity and abundance over our lives.

Hebrews 4:12 says, "For the Word of God is living and powerful, and sharper than any two-edged sword, piercing even to the division of soul and spirit, and of joints and marrow, and is a discerner of the thoughts and intents of the heart."

Why is the Word living and powerful? Because the Word of God is Jesus.

John 1:1 reads, "In the beginning was the Word, and the Word was with God, and the Word was God."

John 1:14 says, "And the Word became flesh and dwelt among us, and we beheld His glory, the glory as of the only begotten of the Father, full of grace and truth."

When we choose to live a sanctified life, meditating day and night in God's Word, fellowshiping with Jesus, our hearts become pure our intentions truthful and our spirits unite and become alive in Christ. Sanctification results in a transformation of our character, which begins with faith in God and results in love.

The Ten Commandments are not some out dated laws that abide in the Old Testament and are only practiced by a few Orthodox Jews. The very same commandments that are written in Exodus chapter 20 are mentioned by Jesus numerous times in the New Testament. (We will discuss this comparison in detail from chapter 4 to 13.) There are many misled Christians who follow the belief that in our day and age, we have no use for the Ten Commandments. Christians have been led to believe that they are now under a 'New Covenant' since the death of Christ.

This is true, but this new covenant mind-set has birthed a cult of false teachings. These false teachings preach that

5

DIVINE SPIRITUAL LAWS

through this 'New Covenant' Christians are now under
'grace'. Misled Christians believe they can live a life of sin
and lawlessness and not even have to ask God for His forgiveness, because of His 'grace'. These types of teachings are
spiritually dangerous and contrary to the Word of God.

One scripture which is often misinterpreted to back up
these types of false teachings is found in Romans 6:14, "For
sin shall not have dominion over you, for you are not under
law but under grace." Paul is teaching here, to be 'under law'
is to be under a system of trying to earn our salvation in our
own strength by obeying the law. To be 'under grace' is to be
justified by God, just as if we had never sinned. Only through
the blood of the Lamb, can we be free from sin and stand
before God justified. When we have the power of Christ living
within us, we are in fellowship with Christ. When we are in
fellowship with Christ and obeying His Word we have power
and knowledge over sin, sin no longer has dominion over our
lives. Even in the Old Testament it was impossible for the
Israelites to obey every one of the 613 commandments (mitz-
voth) of God. The Lord sent His only Son Jesus to save us
from our sins, His yoke is easy and His burden is light. (See
Matthew 11:29–30.) Jesus' yoke (our relationship with Him) is
easy and His burden (Laws, Ten Commandments) are light
in comparison to the heavy burden of the 613 Jewish laws the
Israelites had to obey in the Old Testament. As Christian's
we are under a new covenant with Christ, we are expected
to obey only ten of the 613 commandments from the Old
Testament. These ten laws are the Ten Commandments.

Here is a list of the 613 commandments from the Old
Testament:

- There are 10 commandments pertaining to God
  and His name.

6

What are Divine Spiritual Laws?

- There are 6 commandments pertaining to the Torah and its sanctity.
- There are 5 commandments pertaining to signs and symbols in the Jewish community.
- There are 4 commandments pertaining to prayers and blessings.
- There are 14 commandments pertaining to love and brotherhood.
- There are 13 commandments pertaining to the poor and unfortunate.
- There are 6 commandments pertaining to the treatment of Gentiles.
- There are 23 commandments pertaining to marriage, divorce and family.
- There are 25 commandments pertaining to forbidden sexual relations.
- There are 36 commandments pertaining to the Sabbath and Jewish festivals.
- There are 27 commandments pertaining to dietary laws.
- There are 14 commandments pertaining to business practices.
- There are 19 commandments pertaining to treatment of slaves, servants and employees.
- There are 7 commandments pertaining to vows, oaths and swearing.
- There are 17 commandments pertaining to Sabbatical and Jubilee years.

7

DIVINE SPIRITUAL LAWS

- There are 36 commandments pertaining to Court and Judicial procedure.
- There are 4 commandments pertaining to injuries and damages.
- There are 11 commandments pertaining to property and property rights.
- There are 7 commandments pertaining to criminal laws.
- There are 24 commandments pertaining to punishment and restitution.
- There are 3 commandments pertaining to prophecy.
- There are 46 commandments pertaining to Idolatry, Idolaters and Idolatrous practices.
- There are 7 commandments pertaining to agriculture and animal husbandry.
- There are 3 commandments pertaining to clothing.
- There are 4 commandments pertaining to the firstborn.
- There are 30 commandments pertaining to Kohanim and Levites.
- There are 24 commandments pertaining to T'rumah, tithes and taxes.
- There are 33 commandments pertaining to the Temple, the Sanctuary and sacred objects.
- There are 102 commandments pertaining to Sacrifices and Offerings.

What are Divine Spiritual Laws?

- There are 16 commandments pertaining to Ritual purity and impurity.

- There are 4 commandments pertaining to Lepers and Leprosy.

- There are 7 commandments pertaining to The King.

- There are 10 commandments pertaining to the Nazarites.

- There are 16 commandments pertaining to Wars.

It is impossible for any one man to be able to obey all these laws on a daily basis. The Ten Commandments are achievable in comparison to the 613 commandments in the Old Testament.

Now let's take a look at the word 'grace.' Grace is the unearned favour of God. We cannot earn the favor of God, it is His gift to us and this gift came through the sacrifice of God's only Son, Jesus. We now have the unearned favour of God, 'grace' because of the gift of Christ. This 'grace' is not a licence to live a carnal life and not expect to reap the carnal rewards. Living according to our flesh causes us to be spiritually dead, only 'by the Spirit' which is the Holy Spirit can we put to death the deeds of the body, and live.

> For if you live according to the flesh you will die; but if by the Spirit you put to death the deeds of the body, you will live.
>
> —ROMAN 8:13

> And forgive us our debts, as we forgive our debtors.
>
> —MATTHEW 6:12

DIVINE SPIRITUAL LAWS

What does the Bible say about forgiveness? In Matthew 6:12, Jesus is teaching His disciples how to pray. We are never to discount asking God for His forgiveness of our sins on a daily basis. We are also reminded to forgive those who have sinned against us. Without us humbling ourselves and asking for forgiveness of our sins, we are unable to stand before God and have fellowship with Him. Having unforgiveness in our hearts toward others causes much sorrow in our lives. Unforgiveness leads to sickness, disease, unanswered prayers and broken relationships. When we believe that we never need to come to God and ask for His forgiveness on a daily basis, because we are now under 'grace,' we are denying the power of the death of Jesus on the cross. God is holy, we are not. Only through the blood of Jesus, and forgiveness of our sins, can we even begin to approach the Throne of God. John 14:6, Jesus said to him, "I am the way, the truth, and the life. No one comes to the Father except through Me." This is why God sent His only begotten Son, so that through the sacrifice of Jesus, our fellowship with God could be restored, this is how God always intended it to be from the beginning of time in the Garden of Eden.

> And I will put enmity between you and the woman, and between your seed and her Seed; He shall bruise your head, and you shall bruise His heel.
>
> —GENESIS 3:15

Let's go back to the beginning. In the third chapter of Genesis man has already fallen into temptation. I believe God always knew that man was going to fall into temptation; it was just a matter of time. In this chapter of Genesis, the word 'Seed' has a capital 'S'; this is a reference to Jesus. The word He (Jesus) shall bruise your head (the head of Satan) and you (Satan) shall bruise His (Jesus) heel, are again

10

What are Divine Spiritual Laws?

references to Jesus. God already had a plan for the redemption of man, right from the beginning. His redemptive plan was Jesus. God also has an eternal plan for Satan. Satan is eternally conquered through the death of Jesus on the cross and under His (Jesus) feet/heel. Through the death of Jesus, man's authority and dominion over creation was restored.

Revelation 1:6 tells us, "...and has made us kings and priests to His God and Father, to Him (Jesus) be glory and dominion forever and ever. Amen."

We have been made kings and priests to God, through the death of Jesus on the cross. Adam and Eve handed their right to rule and reign in the Garden of Eden over to Satan. Through the death of Jesus on the cross, Jesus gave the dominion back to man, the 'man' who believes that Jesus is the Son of God, that He died on the cross and rose from the dead. (See Genesis 1:28.)

> And what agreement has the temple of God with idols? For you are the temple of the living God. As God has said: "I will dwell in them and walk among them, I will be their God, and they shall be My people."
> —2 CORINTHIANS 6:16

In Exodus chapter 25, part of the furniture in the Tabernacle was the Ark of the Covenant. The ark was the most sacred of all the furniture in the tabernacle, the reason being the ark represented the presence of God. The ark housed three sacred items, the golden pot of manna (bread) that fell from heaven, the tablets of the law written in stone, (The Ten Commandments) and Aaron's rod that budded. The New Testament teaches us that our bodies are the Temple of God.

DIVINE SPIRITUAL LAWS

First Corinthians 3:16 says, "Do you not know that you are the temple of God and that the Spirit of God dwells in you?"

We no longer need to go through a priest to have access to God as in the Old Testament. Jesus is now our High Priest (Heb. 2:17). God now dwells within us; our spirit has once again been united with God's Spirit through the sacrifice of Jesus. Just as God breathed his 'breath of life' (Holy Spirit) into the nostrils of Adam in Genesis 2:7, the Holy Spirit now dwells and abides in us when we receive Jesus Christ through salvation (Acts 2:3).

As the temple of God, we now house sacred gifts from God. The golden pot of manna, is the Word of God, as Christian's we are to meditate (eat) on His word daily, it is a lamp to our feet and a light to our path (Ps. 119:105). The tablets of the law are the rules the laws by which we live our lives today, the Ten Commandments. The Ten Commandments are God's covenant to us found in the Word of God. Aaron's rod budded, is the authority of God we now have through the death of Jesus, over the enemy, the authority in the name of Jesus. Budding is to show signs of promise. There are hundreds of promises in the Word of God pertaining to Christians. Through our relationship with Christ, learning who God is and what He requires of us through meditating on His word, God will begin to reveal His plan and purpose for us in this world. We were created by God, for God, to be fruitful and multiply and have dominion over the earth.

Genesis 1:28 teaches us, "Then God blessed them, and God said to them, "Be fruitful and multiply; fill the earth and subdue it; have dominion over the fish of the sea, over the birds of the air, and over every living thing that moves on the earth."

What are Divine Spiritual Laws?

And the Lord God commanded the man, saying, "Of every tree of the garden you may freely eat; but of the tree of the knowledge of good and evil you shall not eat, for in the day that you eat of it you shall surely die."

—GENESIS 2:16–17

Even in the history of creation there was one commandment God gave to man. Adam and Eve were not to eat of the tree of the knowledge of good and evil. God only needed to give Adam and Eve one commandment in that time of creation. Adam had the Spirit of God within him (Gen. 2:7), Adam only knew a life with God and fellowship with God on a daily basis, and he hadn't experienced separation from God as yet.

God warned Adam, "for in the day that you eat of it you shall surely die." Adam experienced a spiritual death when he and Eve ate from the tree of the knowledge of good and evil. I don't even think Adam and Eve knew what it meant to die, whether in the spiritual or physical sense. The Spirit of God had made Adam and Eve immortal. Through their disobedience to God, sin entered into the human race. Adam was no longer led by the Spirit of God, but by the lust of the flesh, his once incorruptible body now became corruptible because of sin. Adam choose to live a life without the counsel of God, Adam choose a life where he would now make his own fleshly choices and bear the selfish consequences. Even though our bodies are now mortal, our spirits remain immortal. God sent Jesus to save our immortal spirits; our spirits live on for eternity. We either live eternally in hell or eternally in heaven. The ultimate plan of God is to restore everything back to what He had originally created in the beginning: life in God's Garden (Gen. 2:8).

DIVINE SPIRITUAL LAWS

> All scripture is given by inspiration of God, and is profitable for doctrine, for reproof, for correction, for instruction in righteousness. That the man of God may be complete, thoroughly equipped for every good work.
>
> —2 TIMOTHY 3:16–17

All scripture is "God-breathed," which means all scripture in reality is a product of God's creative breath. God used various men throughout the history of the Bible to physically write down what the Holy Spirit imparted to them, these men were faithful Spirit- filled servants of God. The Word of God is to be used to teach, discipline, correct and instruct the righteous. God is looking for spirit-filled men and women who are fully equipped and complete in the knowledge, wisdom and understanding of His word who are able to exercise the spirit of discernment when required in order to spread the gospel of Christ throughout the world. The law was given to the Israelites by God to make them conscious of their sins, but the Law had no power to overcome sin. Sin is what separates us from the presence of God. We cannot have access to the presence of God when sin is active in our lives. We cannot earn our salvation through obeying the Ten Commandments religiously either. Obeying the Ten Commandments reveals any sin in our lives and brings us to a place of repentance, which then opens a way for our salvation that comes through Christ. Once we have received Jesus Christ as our Lord and Savior our relationship with God our Father is restored and we are able to enter into His presence because of the blood of the Lamb (Jesus' death on the cross).

Chapter 2

COVENANT RELATIONSHIPS

But I will establish My covenant with you; and you shall go into the ark—you, your sons, your wife, and your sons' wives with you.

—GENESIS 6:18

DIVINE SPIRITUAL LAWS

COVENANT CAN BE described as an agreement between two parties. In biblical terms, a covenant is an agreement based on a relationship of commitment between God and His people. No one is forced into a covenant relationship, both parties agree on the terms of the agreement and a covenant is then established between these two parties. In Genesis 6:18, is the first time God mentions a biblical covenant. God promises His protection to Noah and his family through the impending flood, this is God's first installment of the covenant promise to Noah.

> And God said to Noah, "This is the sign of the covenant which I have established between Me and all flesh that is on the earth."
>
> —GENESIS 9:17

Noah was the first man that God made a covenant with on the earth. The sign of the covenant was God's rainbow in the clouds. The rainbow was a sign by which God indicated His intent to restore to Noah and his family what had been lost through Adam and Eve in the Garden of Eden. God made a covenant with Noah and his descendants after the flood, that He would never again destroy ALL flesh through a flood. This covenant still stands today, and is often taken for granted by man. We still witness sporadic floods today, but not ALL flesh is destroyed in these floods. God will never again destroy the whole earth by water, the rainbow is a sign of His covenant promise to man. When we see a rainbow in

16

Covenant Relationships

the clouds, we are reminded of God's covenant with Noah and his descendants. Biblical covenants normally include three elements; the covenants sacrifice, with the shedding of blood, the covenant meal, which establishes the covenant, and the sign of the covenant, which in Noah's case was the rainbow.

> On the same day the Lord made a covenant with Abram, saying; "To your descendants I have given this land, from the river of Egypt to the great river, the River Euphrates."
>
> —GENESIS 15:18

This covenant is the first blood sacrifice covenant. A three-year-old heifer, a three-year-old female goat and a three-year-old ram, a turtle dove and a young pigeon were brought before God and cut in two, down the middle. Only God passed between the sacrificed pieces. The Lord voluntarily made Himself lower than Abram by walking through the cut pieces of animals first. This act by God prefigures the precious gift of His own Son, Jesus, who was to come and die on a degrading cross to save all mankind. This act by God indicated that this was His covenant and that He would be responsible for its administration. Nothing was required of Abram. All Abram had to do was believe God's word. Once Abram believed, he received the promise. The Abrahamic covenant is the Old Testament model for the New Covenant in Jesus Christ.

All we have to do is believe, believe that Jesus is the Son of God and that He died on the cross and rose from the dead and we qualify to receive God's promises for our lives, through salvation.

DIVINE SPIRITUAL LAWS

> As for Me, behold, My covenant is with you, and you
> shall be a father of many nations. No longer shall
> your name be called Abram, but your name shall be
> Abraham; for I have made you a father of many nations.
>
> —GENESIS 17:4–5

In Genesis chapter 15, God had made a covenant with
Abram and promised him and his descendants the land
of Canaan. In Genesis chapter 17, God is ready to give the
sign of the covenant, which would eventually be mani-
fest through the act of circumcision before the birth of
Isaac. God promises Abram that he will be a father of many
nations after Ishmael is born. This is a clear indication that
Abraham had not received the 'promise' from God as yet.
Abram and Sarai had lost hope and faith in waiting for the
promise of God, (Gen. 12:1–3) Sarai decided to take mat-
ters into her own hands. Hagar, Sarai's Egyptian maidservant was given to Abram by Sari and Hagar conceived and
bore Abram a son, Ishmael. Thirteen years after the birth
of Ishmael, God appears to Abram, changes his name to
Abraham, meaning "Father of a Multitude," and changes
Sarai's name to Sarah, meaning, "Princess." A name change
could indicate a change in Abram's character or the defi-
nite call of God upon Abraham's life, which God was now
ready to fulfill. The sign of the covenant which God required
from Abraham was circumcision. Abraham, Ishmael and
all the male men in Abraham's household were circumcised.
Abraham was ninety-nine years old and Ishmael was thirteen years old when they were circumcised. In Jewish custom,
a boy of thirteen has a bar mitzvah and this is the time in his
life when he enters into manhood, he is now responsible for
his own spiritual walk with God, his parents are no longer
accountable for his spiritual walk with the Lord. God waited

Covenant Relationships

until Ismael was thirteen years old before he was circumcised, Ishmael's actions would now be accountable to God and not the responsibility of his father Abraham. Isaac was born after Abraham was circumcised; this was a sign that God chose to establish His covenant with Isaac. Isaac was the son of a freewoman whereas Ishmael was the son of a bondwoman. Isaac represents those that trust in Christ who are the true sons of God whereas Ishmael represents those who are in bondage to the Law (Gal. 4:21–31).

> But my covenant I will establish with Isaac, whom Sarah shall bear to you at this set time next year.
>
> —GENESIS 17:21

> So he was there with the Lord forty days and forty nights; he neither ate bread nor drank water. And He (God) wrote on the tablets the words of the covenant, the Ten Commandments.
>
> —EXODUS 34:28

The Ten Commandments are a summary of the whole covenant mentioned in Exodus chapter 34, between God and Israel. The words of the covenant between God and Israel were written by God on the tables of stone and given to Moses on Mount Sinai.

Moses was on a forty-day fast when he received the words of the covenant, the Ten Commandments. This covenant between God and Moses is known as the Mosaic Covenant. This law was given to Moses 430 years after Abraham's death. God warns that there are consequences for disobeying His commands. Disobedience leads to the promise of a curse and obedience leads to the promise of blessings.

These blessings and curses are explained in detail in Leviticus 26:1–46.

DIVINE SPIRITUAL LAWS

Second Samuel 7:16 tells us, "And your house and your kingdom shall be established forever before you. Your throne shall be established forever." In this passage of Scripture, God reveals His covenant promise with David. In Israel it was generally known that the Messiah was to come from the tribe of Judah and the throne of David. In Matthew 1:1, in the book of the genealogy of Jesus Christ it says, "Jesus Christ, the Son of David, the Son of Abraham." God's covenant promise to David was that He would establish the throne of David forever. The kingdom of God was established through the death of Jesus Christ on the cross and is still growing in numbers today through the church of Jesus Christ.

> But He (Jesus) answered and said, "I was not sent except to the lost sheep of the house of Israel."
> —MATTHEW 15:24

In Matthew 15:24, Jesus is talking to a Gentile woman, she was not Jewish. We now know that God was in a covenant relationship with a chosen generation from the days of Noah. From Noah's bloodline came Abraham, Isaac, Jacob, Joseph, David and eventually Jesus. Scripture teaches us that, Jesus was Jewish.

Matthew 27:11 reads, "Now Jesus stood before the governor. And the governor asked Him, saying, 'Are you the King of the Jews?' Jesus said to him, 'It is as you say.'"

Because of God's covenant relationship with Abraham and his descendants, God was bound by this covenant to send His only Son Jesus to die on a cross first for the lost sheep of the house of Israel. The gospel of Jesus was first offered to the Jews, the Old Covenant people, whom God had a covenant relationship with and then the gospel of Jesus was offered

Covenant Relationships

to the Gentiles, who after accepting the gospel of Jesus, then became the New Covenant people.

> For I am not ashamed of the gospel of Christ, for it is the power of God to salvation for everyone who believes, for the Jew first and also for the Greek.
>
> —ROMANS 1:16

Paul, on entering a city, would first preach the gospel of Jesus Christ in the synagogue and then once the Jews had heard or refused to hear the gospel of Jesus Christ, Paul would then preach to the Gentiles. The first non-Jews to accept the gospel of Christ and be converted were the Samaritan's. The gathering of Israel must precede and prepare for the gathering of the Gentiles. Once we understand the power and the purpose of God's covenant relationship with Israel and how the Gentiles have been "grafted in" we begin to understand and grasp the truth behind the teachings of Jesus in the New Testament.

Romans 11:24 reads, "For if you were cut out of the olive tree which is wild by nature, (Gentiles) and were grafted contrary to nature into a cultivated olive tree, how much more will these, who are natural branches, (Jews) be grafted into their own olive tree?"

Israel's rejection of the gospel of Jesus Christ is temporary. Once all those among the Gentiles have been saved, salvation will again come to a large number of Jews, this will happen the same way that the Gentiles receive Christ, by hearing the Gospel of Jesus Christ preached and receiving Christ by faith.

Romans 11:25–26 teaches us, "…that blindness in part has happened to Israel until the fullness of the Gentiles has come in. And so all Israel will be saved…"

Once God has reaped a vast harvest of Gentiles, then *all*

DIVINE SPIRITUAL LAWS

Israel will be saved. Israel is in a state of 'blindness' at present, until the fullness of the Gentiles has come into the kingdom of God. The Jewish people are the "natural branches" of the olive tree. Once they repent and receive Jesus as their Lord and Savior, they will naturally find their place and purpose in the kingdom of God. Spirit-filled Gentiles are the New Covenant people in Christ. Gentiles do not have the Jewish bloodline or Old Covenant relationship with God. Saved Gentiles accept and receive salvation from the death of Jesus on the cross; they are under a New Covenant, the Covenant of Grace and Salvation, through Christ.

Titus 3:5 tells us, "...not by works of righteousness which we have done, but according to His mercy He saved us, through the washing of regeneration and renewing of the Holy Spirit."

Salvation is the regeneration of the dead spirit of man, through the washing and renewing of the Holy Spirit, making the new man acceptable to God, through Christ. Man is now a new creation:

> Therefore, if anyone is in Christ, he is a new creation, old things have passed away; behold, all things have become new.
>
> —2 CORINTHIANS 5:17

The Jews are the natural heirs of the Old Covenant by birth. The Gentiles are the Spiritual heirs to the New Covenant through Christ. The Jews accepted Abraham as their father and the source of their spiritual blessings. They believed that simply being a descendant of Abraham actually made them righteous. Abraham was a man of faith, the law only came four hundred and thirty years after Abraham. Therefore the true descendants of Abraham and heirs to the promised

Covenant Relationships

blessings are those that live their lives by the principles of faith, just as Abraham did (Gal. 3:6).

"Not with the blood of goats and calves, but with His own blood He entered the Most Holy Place once for all, having obtained eternal redemption. For if the blood of bulls and goats and the ashes of a heifer, sprinkling the unclean, sanctifies for the purifying of the flesh, how much more shall the blood of Christ, who through the eternal Spirit offered Himself without spot to God, cleanse your conscience from dead works to serve the living God?" (Heb. 9:12–14).

Jesus is the Mediator of the New Covenant. We cannot have access to the Father, without going through His Son, Jesus. When a will or testament is drawn up by a lawyer, the will has no legal authority until after the death of the person who had it drawn up. In the same manner, the death of Jesus Christ was necessary for the establishment of the New Covenant. Jesus died once on the cross for the redemption of humanity. He has paid the price for our sins, there is no longer any need for animal sacrifices and rituals as in the Old Testament days, we no longer need to go through a priest to have access and forgiveness of sins from God.

In Matthew 27:51, when Jesus yielded up His Spirit and died on the cross, the veil of the temple was torn in two from top to bottom. This veil was a thick curtain between the Holy Place and the Holy of Holies in the temple. The fact that this veil was torn in two from top to bottom when Christ died indicates this was not an act of man, but of God. The death of Jesus on the cross opened the way for man once again to enter into the presence of God. The New Covenant through Christ fits all three elements of the covenant agreement; Jesus was the blood sacrifice, He established this covenant with His disciples at the last supper and the sign of the New Covenant is the Cross.

23

DIVINE SPIRITUAL LAWS

In summary, the Old Testament mentions five biblical covenants God made with man:

1. The first covenant was God's covenant promise with Noah, that He (God) would never destroy the whole earth again with a flood; the sign of this covenant was the rainbow.

2. The second covenant promise God made was with Abraham, that he would be a father of many nations. Abraham was the founder of the Jewish race. The sign of the covenant was circumcision.

3. The third man God made a covenant promise with was Moses, the Mosaic Covenant, that if Moses and the nation Israel would obey the Ten Commandments, they would live a life of prosperity and have good success, the sign of this covenant was the Ten Commandments.

4. The fourth man God made a covenant promise with in the Old Testament was David. The Davidic Covenant. God promised David that his throne would be established forever, pointing to the coming rulership of Christ, the sign of this covenant was the Messiah (Jesus).

5. The fifth covenant promise God made with Israel was a promise of a Messiah which comes through the birth of Jesus Christ, God's only Son came to save man from his sins by dying on a degrading cross, the sign of this covenant is the Cross. Christ's death on the cross, guarantees our redemption and salvation and access once again into the presence of God.

24

Chapter 3

THE BIRTH OF THE EARLY CHURCH

When the Day of Pentecost had fully come, they were all with one accord in one place. And suddenly there came a sound from heaven, as of a rushing mighty wind, and it filled the whole house where they were sitting. Then there appeared on them divided tongues, as of fire, and one sat upon each of them. And they were all filled with the Holy Spirit and began to speak with other tongues, as the Spirit gave them utterance.

—ACTS 2:1–4

DIVINE SPIRITUAL LAWS

ENTECOST WAS A Jewish festival that was held annually. It was also known as the "Feast of Weeks" or the "Day of First fruits," which was a celebration of the first buds of the harvest. The Jewish men were required to go to Jerusalem three times each year to celebrate these major feasts. Passover was celebrated in spring. Pentecost is seven weeks and a day later after Passover. The Feast of Tabernacles fell at the end of the harvest in the fall. Passover is celebrated as a reminder of how the Israelites were delivered out of Egypt by God, and when the angel of death 'passed' over their homes. The Feast of Tabernacles is a feast in remembrance of the Israelites forty years wandering in the wilderness. Pentecost was also a reminder to the Jewish people of how God revealed the Law to Moses on Mount Sinai, the Ten Commandments.

After the death and resurrection of Jesus, Pentecost took on a whole new meaning to both the Jew and the Gentile. Pentecost now represents the day the Holy Spirit came and the church was born in Jerusalem. The first Christians were Jewish, they were Jesus' disciples. Jesus was crucified the evening before Passover. He was placed in the tomb at the "Feast of Unleavened Bread," (Israel's 'quick' departure from Egypt) and Jesus was raised from the dead during the time of the First fruits. The church was then born on the day of Pentecost. Those who became Christians on the day of Pentecost where the 'first fruits' of a harvest of millions of souls.

26

The Birth of the Early Church

> But you shall receive power when the Holy Spirit has
> come upon you; and you shall be witnesses to Me in
> Jerusalem, and in all Judea and Samaria, and to the
> end of the earth.
>
> —ACTS 1:8

In Acts 1:4, Jesus tells His disciples that they are to wait in Jerusalem for the 'Promise of the Father.' The promise of the Father was the promise of the Holy Spirit. The Holy Spirit could only be imparted to the disciples after the death and resurrection of Jesus. Just like Jesus' ministry on earth began after John the Baptist had baptized Him in the river Jordan (Matt. 3:16–17) and the 'Spirit of God' descended like a dove upon Jesus, the disciples were to wait in Jerusalem for the Baptism of the Holy Spirit from God, before they could begin their ministry. The baptism of the Holy Spirit would now enable the disciples to begin their ministry with the anointing of Christ, they would now have the responsibility to preach and witness Jesus in Jerusalem, Judea and Samaria, and to the end of the earth.

This same responsibility now lies with us as Christians today. Jerusalem represents our community. We are to share Jesus with our direct community members. Judea, represents our whole nation, we are responsible as Christians to share Jesus with our nation. Samaria represents countries abroad. Once we have been obedient to God in witnessing to our own nation then God will open the doors for us to be witnesses of Jesus Christ abroad. To the end of the earth, represents the whole world, once we have been faithful in witnessing Jesus abroad, the Lord will open the door for His gospel to reach the ends of the earth.

DIVINE SPIRITUAL LAWS

> And this gospel of the kingdom will be preached in all
> the world as a witness to all the nations, and then the
> end will come.
>
> —MATTHEW 24:14

Once every nation has heard the gospel of the kingdom
of Christ, then the end will come. The end of this age is
the age we are currently living in, the age of fallen man. As
Christians, we are servants of Christ. In Hebrews 9:14, it
says, our conscience is cleansed from dead works through
the blood of Jesus to serve the living God. As Christians we
are responsible for sharing the gospel of Christ to the lost
souls in this world. We are servants of God, doing His will
on earth, through the power of the Holy Spirit given to us
through the death of Jesus Christ on the Cross, to bring all
men unto salvation.

> Whom heaven must receive until the times of restora-
> tion of all things, which God has spoken by the mouth
> of all His holy prophets since the world began.
>
> —ACTS 3:21

The ultimate restoration will be the return of the church,
the bride of Christ.

Act 3:19–20 reads, "Repent therefore and be converted, that
your sins may be blotted out, so that times of refreshing may
come from the presence of the Lord, and that He may send
Jesus Christ, who was preached to you before…" God is
calling humanity to repentance. Once we start living by His
commandments and stop living a life of compromise, times
of refreshing will come. To be 'refreshed' is to be given new
energy or strength. This refreshing will come from the outpouring of the Holy Spirit upon man, we cannot do anything
worthwhile for Christ in our own strength, only through the

28

The Birth of the Early Church

outpouring of the Holy Spirit upon our lives are we able to accomplish our ministry in Christ. Once we have experience times of refreshing from the presence of the Lord, then God will send His Son, Jesus Christ.

Joel 2:28 reads, "And it shall come to pass afterward that I will pour out My Spirit on all flesh; your sons and your daughters shall prophesy, your old men shall dream dreams, your young men shall see visions." These times of refreshing are the outpouring of the Holy Spirit on all flesh. Just like the former rain, or outpouring of the Holy Spirit upon the disciples at Pentecost. The latter rain will outperform the former rain, and the outpouring of the Holy Spirit will affect every class and race of person. No matter how old, or how young, whether maidservant or wealthy landlord, these people will all see and speak on behalf of God, the prophesies of God, led by the Holy Spirit.

> Be glad then you children of Zion, and rejoice in the Lord your God; for He has given you the former rain faithfully, and He will cause the rain to come down for you—the former rain, and the latter rain in the first month.
>
> — JOEL 2:23

In the climatic patter of Israel, the former rain falls first at the beginning of winter (November/Autumn), and the latter rain falls at the end of winter (April/Spring). The former rain of the Holy Spirit at Pentecost marks the start of the last days. The latter rain of the Holy Spirit, which is still to come, marks the close of the last days, the end of this age. This latter outpouring of the Holy Spirit will refresh and renew many parched souls, which will bring spiritual renewal and a spiritual harvest. Just like the latter rain that falls on the

DIVINE SPIRITUAL LAWS

parched land in Israel at the end of winter brings forth a natural harvest, the latter outpouring of the Holy Spirit on all flesh in the last days, will precede the harvest of souls that will be brought into the kingdom of God.

God multiplies when He restores. Everything that Job lost in the former days of his life, God multiplied in the latter days of Job's life. Job abounded with more blessings from God in the latter days of his life compared to his former days (Job 42:10–12). The plan of God is not only to restore the church to its former state of glory in New Testament times, but God seeks to restore the church to a more powerful and glorious state than anyone has ever seen or experienced in this world.

John 14:12 says, "Most assuredly, I say to you, he who believes in Me, the works that I do he will do also; and greater works than these he will do, because I go to My Father."

When we believe in Jesus, we become a disciple of Christ. A disciple is a follower of the life of Christ. Just because you are a member of a church or an elder or deacon in a specific church, does not necessarily qualify you as a disciple of Christ. Part of Jesus' ministry was to teach. Jesus taught his disciples through parables and the Word of God and He used miracles to display the power of God available to those who believe. We only qualify as disciples of Christ when we are being taught by the Word of God and we are filled and led by the Holy Spirit. The end time move of God, will be preceded by the outpouring of the Holy Spirit (latter rain) on all flesh, all flesh that believes Jesus is the Son of God and that they are His disciples.

Matthew 28:17–20 teaches, as Jesus is speaking, "All authority has been given to Me in heaven and on earth. Go therefore and make disciples of all the nations, baptizing them in the name of the Father and of the Son and of the Holy Spirit: Teaching them to observe all things that

The Birth of the Early Church

I have commanded you; and lo, I am with you always, even to the end of the age. Amen." This was the last command Jesus gave to His disciples, the Great Commission. As followers of Christ, Jesus has officially given us His authority over the ruler of this age. (Satan) We are to make disciples of all nations on the earth, baptizing them in the name of the Father and of the Son and of the Holy Spirit, teaching nations to observe all things Jesus commanded, this is our commission and duty from God as Christians.

Chapter 4

THE FIRST COMMANDMENT

"You shall have no other gods before Me."

—Exodus 20:3

To be a servant of God requires loyalty to God. Our God is a Jealous God. Exodus 34:14 tells us, "For you shall worship no other gods, for the Lord, whose name is Jealous, is a jealous God."

One of God's covenant names is 'Jealous.' The root of the English word *jealous* is zeal. When we are zealous over someone or something, we display signs of enthusiasm, passion and commitment. God displayed His commitment and passion toward us, by sending His only Son, Jesus to die for our sins on a degrading cross. This act of love and passion toward us reveals the heart of God toward man. God is committed to the salvation of His creation, man. God requires our loyalty and belief in Him as our Creator and our only Father.

Let's look at the life of Moses; he was raised in the house of Pharaoh. He was educated in the art of reading and writing in Pharaoh's household. God had a plan and purpose for Moses from the time of his birth. Even though Moses was removed from his parents household as an infant this was the plan of God for his life. Moses received the best education possible during that time in ancient Egypt and he went on to write the first five books of the Bible. Moses was also familiar with the Egyptian customs and laws as well as their gods and idols that they worshiped under Pharaoh's rule. The ten plagues that God send upon Egypt because of Pharaoh's disobedience to the command of God to release the Israelites from under his ruler ship, represented the number of false

The First Commandment

gods that the Egyptians worshiped at that time in history. Through each plague God sent upon Egypt, His power and authority was visibly demonstrated to Pharaoh. Ten plagues were sent by God to give Pharaoh ten opportunities to repent of his evil ways yet each plague caused Pharaoh to harden his heart more and more toward God and the Israelites. (See Exodus 8:15.) When Pharaoh finally gave the command for the Israelites to leave Egypt after the tenth and final plague had killed the first born in every Egyptian home, Moses and the Israelites were very familiar with the false gods and idols of the Egyptian culture. I believe this first commandment that God gave to the Israelites was given on the basis that God knew it was very possible for Israel to slip back into old Egyptian culture and customs and begin to worship the Egyptian gods and idols in place of their true Deliverer and Creator. This first commandment God gave was given to redirect Israel's worship away from Egyptian culture and custom. Israel now had to learn to direct their worship and praise toward one God, Jehovah Elohim, the eternal creator. The Israelites were the only nation at that time in history to worship one God. Other pagan tribes and nations had multiple gods and idols that they worshiped. God set Israel aside amongst all the nations of the earth with this first commandment; "You shall have no other gods before Me."

Other pagan tribes and nations not only had numerous gods which they worshiped but they had made statues and idols of these gods. Israel's God was not visible to the naked eye, Israel was forbidden to make an image or idol to represent their God on earth to man.

Matthew 4:10 says, "Then Jesus said to him, 'Away with you, Satan! For it is written, "You shall worship the Lord your God, and Him only you shall serve.""""

DIVINE SPIRITUAL LAWS

To worship God is to show great respect, adoration and devotion to Him. In Matthew 4:10, Satan comes to tempt Jesus after His forty day fast in the wilderness. Jesus quotes scripture from the Old Testament and the Ten Commandments: "For it is written, 'You shall worship the Lord your God, and Him only shall you serve.'"

Jesus knew the importance of this commandment in His life, Jesus is our example, we are His disciples, we shall worship the Lord our God, and Him only shall we serve. A servant is someone whose duty it is to serve in someone else's house. When we are born again and receive Jesus Christ as our Lord and savior we are now part of the kingdom of God. Jesus was the King of the Jews (Matt. 27:11) a King has a kingdom. Jesus is currently sharing God's throne in heaven, "...who has gone into heaven and is at the right hand of God, angels and authorities and powers having been made subject to Him" (1 Peter 3:22).

Jesus' kingdom is on earth, heaven is retaining Him and His return is dependent upon the readiness of His bride, who is the church of Christ.

> ...whom heaven must receive until the times of restoration of all things, which God has spoken by the mouth of all His holy prophets since the world began.
> —ACTS 3:21

What can be classified as a "god" in our lives? Anything or anyone that has you enslaved to do their will and has your complete adoration and worship is a "god" in your life. If it's the "god" of money that you are serving, you will never have enough money, no matter how hard you work or strive to have the best of everything or how hard you try to store up

36

The First Commandment

riches for yourself here on earth, you will always be a slave to its demonic hold upon your life.

> For the love of money is a root of all kinds of evil, for which some have strayed from the faith in their greediness, and pierced themselves through with many sorrows.
>
> —1 TIMOTHY 6:10

It is not money that is evil, but the "love" of money that is a root of all kinds of evil. This "root" that the Bible is speaking about is the "origin" or the "basic cause." The love of money therefore is the main cause or origin of all kinds of evil. The word evil has many definitions, it means, very immoral, wicked or something harmful and undesirable. When you chose to serve money as a god in your life, you are opening yourself up to harmful, undesirable, wicked behavior, which will cause you to stray from your faith in God and pierce your heart with many sorrows. Another "god" in our lives could be a relationship. We could value a relationship with a husband or a wife or a child above our relationship with God. Our relationship with God is more important than any relationship we can ever imagine having with any one person here on earth.

Only once our relationship is firmly established with God in heaven, can we expect to have meaningful and healthy relationships with family and friends here on earth.

> But if you do not obey Me, and do not observe all these commandments, and if you despise My statutes, or if your soul abhors My judgments, so that you do not perform all My commandments, but break My covenant, I also will do this to you.
>
> —LEVITICUS 26:14–15

DIVINE SPIRITUAL LAWS

Unfortunately there were consequences for Israel not obeying the Ten Commandments from God. Israel would bring upon themselves a flood of curses listed in Leviticus 26:16–26. Today we are not exempt from God's judgment with regards to obeying this first commandment. When we put the trappings and pleasures of this world ahead of serving God, there is a price we will have to pay. In John 12:31, Jesus says, "Now is the judgment of this world; now the ruler of this world will be cast out." This scripture clearly states that Satan is the rules of this world in which we live. When we place the lifestyle of this world, the material objects of this world and the ungodly people in this world ahead of serving God first in our lives, we will be cast out with Satan himself when Jesus comes to judge this world at the end of the age.

For I will look on you favorably and make you fruitful, multiply you and confirm My covenant with you.
—LEVITICUS 26:9

When Israel chose to obey the Lord's commandments, there was a list of blessings that resulted from their obedience to God. These are listed in Leviticus 26:3–13. The same blessings apply to our lives today, when we choose to have no other gods before our Creator. The favor of God becomes evident in our lives; God's favor is His approval upon our lives. We start to bear fruit in every area of our lives. This fruit that we begin to bear will show good results in our work environment, we will begin to bear spiritual fruits, like an open heaven when we pray to God and we will receive the spiritual gifts of the Holy Spirit. The fruit that we begin to bear multiplies and we now begin to live a life that transcends being blessed and prosperous, we

The First Commandment

now being to live a life of abundance. The word abundance means, excess, overflowing and to have in large quantity. As Christian's we should all desire to live a life with excess and abundance, overflowing with the blessings and favor of God.

Chapter 5

THE SECOND COMMANDMENT

"You shall not make for yourself a carved image."

—EXODUS 20:4

DIVINE SPIRITUAL LAWS

I DOLATRY IS TO worship a physical object as a god. The ancient pagan religions in the time of the Israelites were from countries such as Akkad, Mesopotamia and Egypt. Israel was surrounded by pagan tribes who worshiped idols and images called gods. No human artist or sculptor could ever paint or carve an accurate image to represent God in His deity. God forbid the Israelites from creating any image of Him, whether literally or metaphorically. Israel was commanded not to make any carved image or bow down to any carved image or to serve it. The Lord states that He is a jealous God; we discussed this in the previous chapter. It was important in the Old Testament times for the patriarch in the family to obey the Ten Commandments and lead by example. The patriarch of the family was the male head or leader of the family. It was necessary for the patriarch of each family to be in right standing with God as his influence and teachings would affect the whole family to the third and fourth generations.

> Now Laban had gone to shear his sheep, and Rachel
> had stolen the household idols that were her father's.
> —GENESIS 31:19

Laban was Jacob's father-in-law, Laban worshiped pagan gods and according to the ancient law around Haran, the eldest son in the family had the privilege of inheriting the family "gods." Rachel stole these idols either to serve her native religion once she had left her father's house, or to lay

The Second Commandment

claim to them as her inheritance. This passage of scripture is evidence to the fact that idol worship was a major pagan religion in the days of the Israelites. Abraham's father was an idol manufacturer and idol worshiper. When Abraham encountered the true God, he destroyed all his father's idols.

> Little children, keep yourselves from idols. Amen.
>
> —1 JOHN 5:21

We must not allow anyone or anything to lesson our worship, service and devotion to God. We are to live in this world but not partake of the spirit of this world. Remember who the ruler of this world is, we are not to partake of his (Satan's) spirit. Allow God to reveal to you the true spiritual poverty in which this world exists. Once you have an understanding of your inheritance in Christ, all else pales in comparison to what lies ahead for us in the kingdom of God. A life of love, hope, light and peace where God rules eternally. Another form of idolatry is the use of a created thing to assist in our worship of God. I recently had the privilege of visiting the beautiful city of Rome. One aspect of this ancient city that really began to aggravate my spirit was the amount of biblical statues and artwork both painted and sculptured by artists such as Michelangelo portraying Jesus, Mary, and Moses throughout each and every one of the seven hundred churches in Rome.

Every hotel room has a printed picture of the mother Mary and Jesus gazing lovingly into the distance above the beds. After spending a few days in Rome and meditating in the spirit concerning this matter, I came to the revelation and realization that Rome was full of idolatry. Religious people were coming from all over the world during the Christmas period to pay their respects to the "images" of Mary and

DIVINE SPIRITUAL LAWS

Jesus displayed in religious nativity scenes throughout Rome. Tourists were using these idols and images of Christ and Mary to assist in their worship of God. They even bowed down to these carved images and historical artworks when they encountered them in the churches, the streets around Rome and in the Vatican. In the Vatican there are certain doorways you can pass through and it is believed that your sins are forgiven. As Christians we do not need to see Jesus hanging on a cross or Mary holding baby Jesus over a manger to aide us in our worship of Him. Our God is a Spirit; we worship Him in spirit and truth (John 4:24).

> But the hour is coming, and now is, when the true worshipers will worship the Father in spirit and truth; for the Father is seeking such to worship Him.
>
> —JOHN 4:23

No image or idol can be a mediator between God and man. The only true mediator between man and God is Christ. Jesus says in John 14:6, "I am the way, the truth, and the life. No one comes to the Father except through Me." Jesus is our only mediator to enter into the presence of God.

> Then God said, "Let Us make man in Our image, according to Our likeness; let them have dominion over the fish of the sea, over the birds of the air, and over the cattle, over all the earth and over every creeping thing that creeps on the earth."
>
> —GENESIS 1:26

When God made man in His image He made man in the likeness of His form, intellect and Spirit (Gen. 1:27). Adam did not evolve from the form of an ape. The Lord made living creatures before He made man, there was a distinct

The Second Commandment

difference between the creation of living creatures and man, Adam was made in God's image (Gen. 1:24–25). God created man to have dominion over His kingdom on earth. Man was to rule and subdue everything God had created, including the forceful satanic realm, which would soon reveal itself to Adam and Eve in the Garden of Eden in the form of a serpent.

He who has seen Me has seen the Father; so how can you say, "Show us the Father?"

—JOHN 14:9

Jesus is speaking to Philip in this scripture. Jesus clearly states that the disciples have seen the Father, now that they have seen Him. Only God is permitted to make an image of His likeness and He chose to make this image through His creation of man. David says in Psalm 139:14, "I will praise You, for I am fearfully and wonderfully made."

We are unique to God, no human being has the same thumb print, every hair on our head is numbered by God, we are truly fearfully and wonderfully made by God.

And it came to pass, at the time of the offering of the evening sacrifice, that Elijah the prophet came near and said, "Lord God of Abraham, Isaac, and Israel, let it be known this day that You are God in Israel and I am Your servant, and that I have done all these things at Your word. Hear me, O Lord, hear me, that this people may know that You are the Lord God, and that You have turned their hearts back to You again." Then the fire of the Lord fell and consumed the burnt sacrifice, and the wood and the stones and the dust, and it licked up the water that was in the trench. Now when all the people saw it, they fell on their faces; and they said, "The Lord, He is God! The Lord, He is God!" And

45

DIVINE SPIRITUAL LAWS

> Elijah said to them, "Seize the prophets of Baal! Do
> not let one of them escape!" So they seized them; and
> Elijah brought them down to the Brook Kishon and
> executed them there.
>
> —1 KINGS 18:36–40

This passage of scripture reflects on Elijah's victory over
the prophets of Baal on Mount Carmel. Elijah was outnum-
bered by the prophets of Baal 450 to 1. Elijah challenges the
prophets of Baal and their gods. Each lays a sacrificed bull
cut in pieces on a wooden altar. Elijah proposes that the
prophets of Baal are to call on their gods and he will call on
his God, and the God who answers by fire, He is God. We
know how this story ends, even when the odds are stacked
against Elijah after the altar he builds made out of wood
and stone and the burnt sacrifice are saturated with water
three times over, God still consumes the entire altar, sacrifice
and water with fire, the burnt sacrifice, the wood, the stones
and the dust are all licked up by the flames. The prophets of
Baal are then seized and executed. This account of Elijah's
faith in God, clearly displays God's standard with regards to
idol worship. The idol worshipers were executed. Israel now
understood that there was a price to pay for disobeying the
commandments of God. The Lord used this public defeat over
the prophets of Baal to display His judgment on the topic of
idol worship to the nation of Israel. The consequences were
death, both a spiritual and physical death.

> Then Jesus said to him, "Away with you, Satan! For it
> is written, you shall worship the Lord your God, and
> Him only you shall serve."
>
> —MATTHEW 4:10

The Second Commandment

Jesus knew that the earthly power that Satan was offering Him would only be temporary. Jesus rebukes Satan first and then quotes the Word of God "it is written." Jesus confirms that we are only to worship the Lord our God. When the enemy comes to us and offers us the temptations of this world, our first response should be to rebuke Satan and then quote the Word of God to him. Anything Satan offers you in this world will always come at a price; normally the price of your salvation. Everything he tempts you with will have no lasting value in this world. God offers us eternal life, we cannot take riches with us when we die we can only take our spirits which live on for eternity.

> Behold, I have set before you today a blessing and a curse: the blessing, if you obey the commandments of the Lord your God which I command you today; and the curse, if you do not obey the commandments of the Lord your God, but turn aside from the way which I command you today, to go after other gods which you have not known.
>
> —DEUTERONOMY 11:26–28

This same principle applies in our lives today. We have a choice as servants of Christ. We either choose to obey the word of the Lord or we choose to follow the temptations of this carnal world we live in. Our actions and choices will determine whether we live a life filled with God's blessing and favor or a life plagued by misery and defeat, under a curse. The decision lies with us, there is no gray area or middle ground in the Bible, the Word of God is emphatic with regards to the consequences of this second commandment, we either choose to worship God or Satan.

Chapter 6

THE THIRD COMMANDMENT

"You shall not take the name of the Lord your God in vain."

—Exodus 20:7

DIVINE SPIRITUAL LAWS

God's name and His character are inseparable, "You shall be holy, for I the Lord your God am holy" (Lev. 19:2). God is holy and we are to be imitators of God. To be holy is to separate yourself from everything that is profane and defiling in this world and dedicate yourself to everything that is holy and pure in the sight of God.

The name of God is disrespected in magic, misused under oath in courts of law and used in vain on primetime television daily in America 95 percent of the time. To use the Lord's name in vain is to use His name in a way that shows a lack of respect for Him as God.

> And the tongue is a fire, a world of iniquity. The tongue is so set among our members that it defiles the whole body, and sets on fire the course of nature; and it is set on fire by hell.
>
> —JAMES 3:6

The tongue is referred to as a fire, how do we put out a fire? We throw water on it. No man can tame the tongue, except the Holy Spirit, when a person is filled with the Holy Spirit it is like holy water from heaven cleansing a person's soul and mind and mouth from within. We need to constantly be aware of what comes out of our mouths. The tongue is set on fire by hell, this means that when we talk about people behind their backs or slander a person's character or use the name of the Lord in vain, our words are set on fire by hell itself and Satan. We defile our whole body when our words

The Third Commandment

are motivated by the fire of hell. Think of how quickly a fire spreads and how much damage it can cause in such a short space of time. Our negative and faithless words that proceed out of our mouths spreads just like a fire and causes severe damage to the lives of innocent people.

> Then God said, "Let there be light," and there was light.
> —GENESIS 1:3

When God created the heavens and the earth, it was a process of placing everything that He created in complete order and beauty, compared to the original state of chaos the earth was in, without form. The most powerful creative tool God used was His word. God said, "Let there be light".

God's first divine command was to speak light into existence in the presence of complete darkness that was on the face of the deep. God saw that the light was good. He then proceeded to divide the light from the darkness, creating a balance between the light and darkness. As followers of Christ, our words we speak bear the same authority and impact upon creation today. Our words can either built up or destroy a person, a business, a marriage or our own lives. Every word we utter is written down by God's angels and records of these words are kept in the archives of heaven until the day of judgment (1 Pet. 4:17). We need to choose our words carefully and speak words of life and not death.

> Let it be known to you all, and to all the people of Israel, that by the name of Jesus Christ of Nazareth, whom you crucified, whom God raised from the dead, by Him this man stands here before you whole. This is the stone which was rejected by you builders, which has become the chief cornerstone. Nor is there salvation

DIVINE SPIRITUAL LAWS

in any other, for there is no other name under heaven
given among men by which we must be saved.

—ACTS 4:10–12

In this scripture, Peter and John are addressing the
Sanhedrin concerning the use of the name of Jesus and the
healing of a lame man. The Sanhedrin was a gathering of
officials, a Jewish religious senate. These Sanhedrin knew
that Peter and John had not received any formal education
in the rabbinical schools and marveled at the boldness with
which these disciples spoke and taught in the name of Jesus.
These Jewish officials recognized the power in the name of
Jesus, and they commanded the disciples not to speak or
teach in the name of Jesus.

Acts 4:18 says, "So they called them and commanded them
not to speak at all nor teach in the name of Jesus." Every
Christian knows that there is power in the name of Jesus.

For where two or three are gathered together in My
name, I am there in the midst of them.

—MATTHEW 18:20

When we come together in the name of Jesus, His presence is in the midst of us, to perform miracles, save souls
and set the captives free.

And she will bring forth a Son, and you shall call His
name Jesus, for He will save His people from their sins.

—MATTHEW 1:21

The name 'Jesus' means, "Yahweh is Salvation." Yahweh is
one of the names by which God revealed Himself to Israel.
Jesus is Salvation. Every time we say, "Jesus" we are con-
firming that He is our Salvation, our only true Savior. God

52

The Third Commandment

revealed Himself and His character to the nation of Israel through His various names. Jehovah Elohim means, the eternal creator (Gen. 2:4–25). Jehovah Jireh means, the Lord our provider (Gen. 22:8–14). Jehovah Shalom means, the Lord our peace (Judg. 6:24). There are another thirteen names by which Israel knew the Lord, He revealed His nature to them as The Lord my shepherd, The Lord our maker, The Lord our righteousness to mention a few. God places much importance on a name. When we choose a name for a child, we must carefully consult the Lord concerning this matter. When you call your child 'Donovan' which means 'Dark warrior' you are confessing that he is a 'Dark warrior' every time you call him by name. The name 'David', on the other hand means, 'Beloved'. The name Jethro means abundance.

When choosing a girl's name:

- the name *Hannah* means gracious
- the name *Ruth* means friend.

And the Israelite woman's son blasphemed the name of the Lord and cursed; and so they brought him to Moses...Then they put him in custody, that the mind of the Lord might be shown to them. And the Lord spoke to Moses, saying, "Take outside the camp him who has cursed; then let all who heard him lay their hands on his head, and let all the congregation stone him."

—LEVITICUS 24:11–14

The penalty for blasphemy in the Old Testament was death. Whether you were a stranger or born in the land of Israel and you blasphemed the name of the Lord you were put to death, it was considered a serious offence.

DIVINE SPIRITUAL LAWS

Today we cannot go around stoning people to death for using the Lord's name in vain, but we can warn them that there will be spiritual consequences for breaking this commandment. These blasphemers will be held accountable to God for using His name in vain and showing no respect for their creator, they will stand before God Himself and be held accountable to Him. I personally believe that a person who can use the Lord's name in vain doesn't have a relationship with God or know Him. The Lord will not hold him guiltless who takes His name in vain. When you know the true character and nature of someone who is good and holy, you will not be able to defile this person's character through blasphemy. Those who practice blasphemy desperately need to have an encounter with Jesus Christ and become born again.

"In this manner, therefore, pray: Our Father in heaven, Hallowed be Your name."

—MATTHEW 6:9

Here Jesus is teaching His disciples how to pray to God the Father. Jesus addresses God as, Our Father in heaven. Jesus has a very intimate relationship with God, His Father. Hallowed is to make holy, to be greatly respected and worshiped. Jesus demonstrates that when we pray to God, we are to come before Him with an attitude of worship and reverence. God is in heaven we are on earth. When we come before our Father in humility and prayer and glorify His name, He will exalt us before men, "Humble yourselves in the sight of the Lord, and He will lift you up" (James 4:10).

In the New Testament, Christian slaves who served unbelieving masters had to show respect for their masters so that their faith would not be spoken against in an act of blasphemy. These slaves had to set a good example as Christians;

54

there was no room for hypocrisy. Many unbelievers today will not even consider Christianity as their choice of religion because of Christians who have lived a hypocritical lifestyle without coming to a place of repentance before God. We need to set a good example as Christians and make sure we practice what we preach to others, this was a prerequisite for those who converted to Christianity in the early church.

First Timothy 6:1 teaches us, "Let as many bondservants as are under the yoke count their own masters worthy of all honor, so that the name of God and His doctrine may not be blasphemed."

Chapter 7

THE FOURTH COMMANDMENT

"Remember the Sabbath day, to keep it holy."

—EXODUS 20:8

DIVINE SPIRITUAL LAWS

THE SABBATH IS a holy day, set aside to God. It is a day of rest and worship unto God. The word Sabbath derives from the Hebrew word Shabbat which means "to cease." The Israelites were to cease from whatever they were occupied with on the Sabbath and they were to honor God with rest and worship on the seventh day. God had already established this pattern in creation, God worked for six days when He created the heavens and the earth and everything in it and He rested on the seventh day (Gen. 2:2). The Sabbath was a sign of God's covenant relationship with Israel, those who observed the Sabbath would enjoy its divine blessings from God. The Sabbath also set the Israelites aside from amongst the pagan tribes of their times, the Sabbath delivered the Israelites from the seven day work week which Egypt was accustomed to. The Israelites were not only to observe the weekly Sabbath. There was the Sabbath Year which occurred once every seven years.

> Six years you shall sow your land and gather in its produce, but the seventh year you shall let it rest and lie fallow, that the poor of your people may eat; and what they leave, the beasts of the field may eat. In like manner you shall do with your vineyard and your olive grove.
>
> —EXODUS 23:10–11

Every seventh year the land was to rest and lie fallow, this gave the land an opportunity to rest from seed-time

The Fourth Commandment

and harvest-time and replenish the soil with nutrients and organisms for the following six years of harvesting that lay ahead. Any trees or crops that grew on the land during the Sabbath Year were made available to the poor to eat and for the roaming beast of the fields to feed on. There was also the Year of Jubilee, the fiftieth year that followed seven Sabbath years, and which proclaimed liberty to those who were servants because of debt and land was returned to the former owners (Lev. 25:8–17).

> "Work shall be done for six days, but the seventh is the Sabbath of rest, holy to the Lord. Whoever does any work on the Sabbath day, he shall surely be put to death."
>
> —Exodus 31:15

Disobeying the Sabbath in the Old Testament was punishable by death. The Sabbath was a sign between God and the children of Israel forever. This sign of the Sabbath was God's covenant with Israel throughout their generations that they would know that God was the God who sanctified them.

> And He said to them, "The Sabbath was made for man, and not man for the Sabbath. Therefore the Son of Man is also Lord of the Sabbath."
>
> —Mark 2:27–28

In this passage of Scripture, Jesus and His disciples were passing through the grain fields on the Sabbath and as they walked the disciples began to pluck the heads of grain, because they were hungry. The disciples were not guilty of breaking any spiritual law concerning the Sabbath by plucking the heads of grain. They were only guilty of breaking the Sabbath according to the Pharisees interpretation of the Sabbath.

59

DIVINE SPIRITUAL LAWS

Jesus enlightens the Pharisees with two new principles concerning the Sabbath.

Firstly, God intended the Sabbath to be for the spiritual and physical benefit of the Israelites. The Rabbis had composed countless man-made rules to protect the Sabbath and it was one of these man-made rules concerning the Sabbath that the disciples had broken. Secondly, Jesus states His equality with God when He says, "the Son of Man is also Lord of the Sabbath." Because the Sabbath was made for man and not man for the Sabbath, Jesus is the Son of God and is also Lord of the Sabbath. Jesus was with God when God created the heavens and the earth in the beginning (John 1:1–4) and Jesus rested with God on the seventh day. He knew the true meaning and purpose of the Sabbath from the beginning of time. Jesus had the revelation of the true Sabbath set in place by God, opposed to the religious version of the Sabbath the Pharisees imposed on the Jewish community.

> I was in the Spirit on the Lord's Day, and I heard behind me a loud voice, as of a trumpet.
>
> —REVELATION 1:10

The Lord's Day in Christianity is known as the first day of the week, Sunday. Christians gather on a Sunday to worship and praise the Lord and it is considered a day of rest. Christians commemorate Sunday as the day Christ rose from the dead and appeared to His disciples.

> Then the same day at evening, being the first day of the week, when the doors were shut where the disciples were assembled, for fear of the Jews, Jesus came and stood in the midst, and said to them, "Peace be with you."
>
> —JOHN 20:19

The Fourth Commandment

There used to be a time in South Africa when all the stores closed on a Sunday, you could not buy food, liquor or petrol everything shut down to honor our faith and belief in God on a Sunday. We have become like the pagan religions of old, we work seven-day weeks without a rest, we are driven by greed, selfishness and over indulgence. As Christians we are to 'remember the Sabbath day,' to 'remember' is to bear something or someone in mind and we are to keep this Sabbath day 'holy.' The word holy can be defined as 'dedicated to God.' I believe that remembering the Sabbath day and keeping it holy from a Christian's perspective, is to cease from all labor on the Sabbath and to make a conscious effort to be righteous before God and to honor God in prayer and thanksgiving, it is not a day to be bound up by religious rituals, it is a day of rest and restoration and a day to receive from God. As Christian's we do not serve God for "religious" purposes. We have a "relationship" with God and serve Him because we love Him not out of duty or religious fear. Jesus healed many sick people on the Sabbath. (Luke 14:4) If you require healing in your body, set time aside and seek God on the Sabbath day and trust God for your healing on the Sabbath . Let us take a step back and reflect on what Jesus says in Matthew 11:28–30, "Come to Me, all you who labor and are heavy laden, and I will give you rest. Take My yoke upon you and learn from Me, for I am gentle and lowly in heart, and you will find rest for your souls. For My yoke is easy and My burden is light."

In Christianity our sanctification comes through Christ. Jesus calls for a relationship with us.

Chapter 8

THE FIFTH COMMANDMENT

"Honor your father and your mother."

—Exodus 20:12

DIVINE SPIRITUAL LAWS

A BIBLE-BASED FAMILY IS the key component to a healthy society. To honor means to show respect, to glorify and to exalt.

Israelite children were instructed to honor their mother and father in order to live a long and prosperous life in the Promised Land that God was giving them. Here is an account of the sons of Eli, who had no respect for the Lord or for their earthly father Eli.

> Now Eli was very old, [ninety-eight years] and he heard everything his sons did to all Israel, and how they lay with the woman who assembled at the door of the tabernacle of meeting. So he said to them, "Why do you do such things? For I hear of your evil dealings from all the people. No, my sons! For it is not a good report that I hear. You make the Lord's people transgress. If one man sins against another, God will judge him. But if a man sins against the Lord, who will intercede for him?" Nevertheless they did not heed the voice of their father, because the Lord desired to kill them.
>
> —1 SAMUEL 2:22–25

Eli was a priest in the temple at Shiloh in a time in Israel's history when the temple had been desecrated and the priesthood was corrupt and immoral. Eli's own sons were wicked and demanded the choice meat of the sacrifice for themselves before it was offered to God, this act was considered an act of robbing God, which would cost them their lives.

The Fifth Commandment

So the messenger answered and said, "Israel has fled before the Philistines, and there has been a great slaughter among the people. Also your two sons, Hophni and Phinehas, are dead; and the ark of God has been captured."

—1 SAMUEL 4:17

God's desire was to kill Hophni and Phinehas because of their disrespect toward God and Eli. Their lives were brought to an early and tragic end. Eli died on the same day as his sons when he heard that the ark of God had been captured (God's presence was no longer with Israel) Eli fell off his seat backwards and broke his neck. The penalty for not honoring a mother or a father in the Old Testament was death (Exod. 21:15–17). Israelites were expected to show respect for the elderly, they were to rise before the gray-headed, and they were to honor the presence of an old man (Lev. 19:32).

"Now there stood by the cross of Jesus His mother, and His mother's sister, Mary the wife of Clopas, and Mary Magdalene. When Jesus therefore saw His mother, and the disciple whom He loved standing by, He said to His mother, 'Woman behold your son!' Then He said to the disciple, 'Behold your mother!' And from that hour that disciple took her to his own home."

—JOHN 19:25–27

In this passage of Scripture, Jesus is dying on the cross and is on the verge of releasing His Spirit to God when He looks down and sees His mother Mary standing at the foot of the cross. He sees her pain and suffering as she is about to lose a Son. In that moment, He tells her to behold her son, which is the disciple standing next to her, and He says to the disciple, "Behold your mother!" Even in death, Jesus displayed

DIVINE SPIRITUAL LAWS

emotions of love and compassion toward his earthly mother. He made sure she was taken care of on earth even after He went to heaven to be with His Father.

> Train up a child in the way he should go, And when he is old he will not depart from it.
>
> —PROVERBS 22:6

As parents we have the responsibility of training our children in the way they should go. To "train up" a child is to lovingly invest whatever wisdom, love and discipline we have received from God, into a child's life so that they become fully committed to God. "In the way he should go," means to train a child according to the child's unique personality, gifts and aspirations he or she might have. It also means to train a child to avoid whatever tendencies he or she might have that would steer them away from their commitment to God. If a child has a weak will or suffers from depression or lack of discipline, it is the parent's responsibility to direct the child according to the Word of God in love. Training a child up in this manner will ensure that he or she will not depart from it when they are older.

In today's society, children are rebellious, unloving, and angry and display signs of violence and rage toward people in society. All these symptoms are a result of children coming out of broken, ungodly homes or homes that are filled with violence and abuse. The foundation for a healthy society is based on solid, stable Christian family homes, where children are taught the Word of God, where husbands and wives respect one another and where the family fellowships at a local church together every Sunday. Children learn by example, when they see their mother and father honor God and each other, they will follow suite. One of the main causes of divorce is a

The Fifth Commandment

hardened heart toward God and then toward one another. The only way to change the course of your marriage if it is heading toward divorce is to commit to a seven-day fast. Fasting changes us not God. When we humble ourselves before God through prayer and fasting we enable the Holy Spirit to work miracles in our lives and marriages. God never intended for a man and a woman to divorce. Jesus speaking to the Pharisees says, "Moses, because of the hardness of your hearts, permitted you to divorce your wives, but from the beginning it was not so" (Matt. 19:8).

The Lord desires for us to have happy families, to be fruitful and multiply and to live a life honoring Him and one another, so that our days on this earth may be fruitful, blessed and prosperous. The Devil will use unforgiveness, divorce and adultery to destroy the family unit and the natural creative order created by God in the Garden of Eden. The natural order of creation is for one man to marry one woman and they are to be fruitful and multiply and fill the earth and subdue it. (See Genesis 1:27–28.) This is the way God ordained it to be from the beginning of time in the Book of Genesis.

Chapter 9

THE SIXTH COMMANDMENT

"You shall not murder."

—Exodus 20:13

DIVINE SPIRITUAL LAWS

To murder is to take a human life unlawfully. Because man is made in the image of God (Gen. 1:27) man has morals, spiritual values and reason, it is these unique qualities that separate man from animals. Because man is made in God's image, God forbid men to kill one another unlawfully.

> Now Cain talked with Abel his brother; and it came to pass when they were in the field, that Cain rose up against Abel his brother and killed him.
>
> —GENESIS 4:8

This is the first account of murder in the Bible. God did not respect Cain's offering that he made to God and this made Cain angry and his countenance fell. The reason why God respected Abel's offering was because Abel brought the firstborn of his flock and of their fat, whereas Cain just brought an offering of the fruit of the ground, he didn't even bring the best of the fruit or the first fruits of the ground as an offering to the Lord. Cain showed disrespect toward God with his offering, therefore God did not respect Cain's offering. The root of the act of murder is anger. Cain harbored anger toward God, he hardened his heart toward God and his brother Abel and the result was murder.

> Then the Lord said to Cain, "Where is Abel your brother?" He said, "I do not know. Am I my brothers keeper?"
>
> —GENESIS 4:9

The Sixth Commandment

When God asked Cain where his brother was, God was giving Cain an opportunity to repent of his sin. God knew what Cain had done; God could hear the voice of Abel's blood crying out to Him from the ground. No matter how awful the sin, God will always give us an opportunity to repent and receive His forgiveness from our sins.

> If men fight, and hurt a woman with child, so that she gives birth prematurely, yet no harm follows, he shall surely be punished accordingly as the woman's husband imposes on him, and he shall pay as the judges determine. But if any harm follows, then you shall give life for life.
>
> —EXODUS 21:22–23

Even in the womb an unborn child was considered a human life in the Old Testament. If a pregnant mother gave birth prematurely as a result of two men fighting, there was a price to pay by the offender, if the pregnant woman's child died, the offender was put to death, a life for a life.

> Before I formed you in the womb I knew you; before you were born I sanctified you; I ordained you a prophet to the nations.
>
> —JEREMIAH 1:5

God knew us before we were formed in our mother's womb, before we were born God set us apart for His appointed plan and purpose, just like Jeremiah was to be a prophet to the nations, we have a special calling from God upon our lives from before we were placed in our mother's womb. To abort a pregnancy is considered an act of murder upon an innocent life according to the Word of God. Satan uses fear, confusion and lies from the pit of hell to convince a pregnant mother

71

DIVINE SPIRITUAL LAWS

to abort her unborn baby. God has an appointed plan and purpose for our lives and Satan has his plan and purpose for our lives, if Satan can end a human life in the womb he will use every lie, excuse and fear possible to encourage a pregnant mother to abort her baby before he or she is even born. If Satan can end a life before it has truly begun he has succeeded in destroying the plan of God in an individuals life. The penalty for murder in the Old Testament was death, a life for a life.

> The Lord is a man of war; The Lord is His name.
> —EXODUS 13:3

A man of war is a warrior, the Lord fought many battles for Israel, many of Israel's enemies knew that when they declared war against Israel they declared war against God. The Lord gave a battle plan to Joshua on how to conquer Jericho in Joshua 6:1–27. The Lord is not only a man of war: He has Commanders in His army from heaven who are commissioned by Him to do His will (Josh. 5:13–15). There is a distinct difference between people losing their lives in war, in self-defense or through capital punishment in the Old Testament opposed to being murdered. War, self-defense and capital punishment are considered lawful ways to die, whereas murder is unlawful with regards to this sixth commandment from the Lord.

> You have heard that it was said to those of old, "You shall not murder, and whoever murders will be in danger of the judgment." But I say to you that whoever is angry with his brother without a cause shall be in danger of the judgment.
> —MATTHEW 5:21–22

The Sixth Commandment

In this scripture, Jesus elaborates on the sixth commandment from the Old Testament. He reveals that murder is not only an action committed by the murderer, but that it extends to the evil thoughts and words of unrighteous men. To call someone 'stupid' is to show contempt toward their mind and to call someone a 'fool' is to show contempt toward their character. These feelings and thoughts of contempt toward our brethren may be nurtured by a hardened heart and will result in murder, unless a person approaches his brother and reconciles with him before God and man.

> The thief does not come except to steal, and to kill, and to destroy, I have come that they may have life, and that they may have it more abundantly.
>
> —JOHN 10:10

The positive side of this sixth commandment is that God is the giver of life. Satan only comes into our lives to steal, kill and destroy everything we love and own. Jesus says He came that we may have life, and that we may have it more abundantly. Life is the ability to grow, breathe, reproduce and exist.

God gave us this ability when he made man in the beginning in the Garden of Eden (Gen. 1:28). Abundance is to exist in large quantity, excess or plentiful. Jesus came so that we can live a life 'more abundantly' Jesus came to restore to man what the Father had given to Adam in the garden of Eden (dominion and prosperity) which Satan deceitfully stole away when he tempted Adam and Eve in the Garden of Eden.

Chapter 10

THE SEVENTH COMMANDMENT

"You shall not commit adultery."

—EXODUS 20:14

DIVINE SPIRITUAL LAWS

A DULTERY IS WHEN a married person has sexual intercourse with a person who is not his or her husband or wife. God never intended for man to experience divorce, from the beginning He made one man Adam for one woman Eve.

> And the Lord God caused a deep sleep to fall on Adam, and he slept, and He took one of his ribs, and closed up the flesh in its place. Then the rib which the Lord God had taken from man He made into a woman, and He brought her to the man. And Adam said: "This is bone of my bones and flesh of my flesh; she shall be called Woman, because she was taken out of Man." Therefore a man shall leave his father and mother and be joined to his wife, and they shall become one flesh. And they were both naked, the man and his wife, and were not ashamed.
>
> —GENESIS 2:21–25

The Lord values marriage, the Bible starts with a marriage in the beginning between Adam and Eve and ends with marriage in the Book of Revelation between Christ and His Bride, the church. God saw that Adam was alone and needed a helper (Genesis 2:18) once Adam had fallen into a deep sleep, the Lord took one of Adams ribs and made woman. Woman was made from the rib of man, not the foot or the fist or the head but from his side, woman was created to be a helper to man and comparable (similar) to him. When a

76

The Seventh Commandment

man and woman unite in marriage, the man leaves his father and mother and is now joined to his wife. This implies he is now passionately and permanently joined to his wife. They became one flesh when they consummated their marriage through the act of sexual intercourse. Marriage is a covenant relationship between a man and a woman. Adam and Eve were not ashamed of their nakedness in the Garden of Eden. They saw one another through the eyes of the Lord they saw no flaws or faults in each other's personalities or bodies, they were pure and innocent before the Lord and they knew no sin.

> Then David sent messengers, and took her; and she came to him, and he lay with her, for she was cleansed from her impurity; and she returned to her house. And the woman conceived; so she sent and told David, and said, "I am with child."
>
> —2 SAMUEL 11:4–5

This is the well-known story of David and Bathsheba and her husband Uriah. David committed adultery when he took Uriah's wife and lay with her while Uriah was at war. There was no reason for David to be in Jerusalem at this time of the year, it was spring time and all the kings were out to war. David's rightful place should have been with his armies fighting against the Ammonites in Rabbah. Instead, he was idly walking about his roof top one cool spring evening when he saw beautiful Bathsheba taking a bath. He sends for Bathsheba and lies with her, knowing that she is the wife of Uriah the Hittite. David knowingly committed adultery. Once David finds out that Bathsheba is pregnant with his child, he sends for Uriah to come home from the battle field. His plan is for Uriah to lay with his wife Bathsheba and then

DIVINE SPIRITUAL LAWS

Uriah will not be suspicious of his wife's pregnancy nine months later.

Uriah comes back to Jerusalem, but he doesn't go home, he sleeps at the door of the king's house. David gives Uriah a few more days in Jerusalem, David eats and drinks with Uriah and gets Uriah drunk hoping he will go home to his wife, Bathsheba. Instead, Uriah falls asleep with the servants of his lord and does not go home. David is now desperate, he sends a letter to Joab and sends orders for Uriah to be sent to the forefront of the hottest battle so that he may be struck down and die. Now David is guilty of breaking two of the commandments of God, he has committed adultery and he has committed murder.

> And the Lord struck the child that Uriah's wife bore to David, and it became ill. David therefore pleaded with God for the child, and David fasted and went in and lay all night on the ground. So the elders of his house arose and went to him, to raise him up from the ground. But he would not, nor did he eat food with them. Then on the seventh day it came to pass that the child died.
>
> —2 SAMUEL 12:15–18

Even after David had confessed to Nathan that he had sinned against the Lord, there was still a price David had to pay for his transgressions. Because David despised the commandment of the Lord, he had given his enemies great occasion to blaspheme the name of the Lord, the price he would have to pay would be the life of his firstborn child born from Bathsheba. After seven days of fasting and pleading with God after the birth of the child, the baby dies. David arises from the ground, washes and anoints himself and changes his clothes and goes to the house of the Lord to worship God, then he goes home

The Seventh Commandment

and requests that food be sent to him. His servants are confused, while his child was alive, David fasted and prayed and now that the child is dead, he arises and anoints himself, worships God, breaks his fast and eats a meal.

David's response is, "But now he is dead; why should I fast? Can I bring him back again? I shall go to him, but he shall not return to me" (2 Samuel 12:23).

David had the revelation that he could not bring his dead son back to him, but that he could one day join his son in heaven. David understood the true meaning of repentance before God. God then blessed both David and Bathsheba with another son, his name was Solomon, and the Lord loved him (2 Sam. 12:24–25). Repentance before God always brings restoration.

> And it came to pass after these things that his master's wife cast longing eyes on Joseph, and she said, "Lie with me." But he refused and said to his master's wife, "Look, my master does not know what is with me in the house, and he has committed all that he has to my hand."
>
> —GENESIS 39:7–8

Here is an account in the life of Joseph were he could have committed adultery with Potiphar's wife, but he refused her. The Bible mentions that Joseph was "handsome in form and appearance" (v. 6). Potiphar's wife hounded Joseph day by day to lie with her, yet he still refused her. While Joseph was in the house working alone one day, Potiphar's wife caught him by his garment so that he would lay with her; instead, he left his garment in her hands and fled outside. She then used his garment against him as false evidence claiming to

DIVINE SPIRITUAL LAWS

her husband, that Joseph had lain with her to mock her, as Joseph was a Hebrew man and she was an Egyptian woman.

Potiphar believed his wife and Joseph was sent to prison, no ordinary prison, he was sent to a prison where all the king's prisoners were confined. Even though Joseph was innocent, he was punished by man, but not by God. This was a test in Joseph's life, a test of his character, his morals and his faith in God. The Lord saw that Joseph was a faithful and honest man and even while he was in prison, God was with Joseph, He gave him favor and showed him mercy. All the prisoners were under Joseph's authority and the Lord made Joseph prosper in whatever he did. We know how this story ends, Joseph eventually interprets Pharaoh's disturbing dream for him. Pharaoh is so impressed by Joseph and recognizes that he has the Spirit of God in him to interpret his dream, that he puts Joseph second in charge to him over all of Egypt.

This account in the life of Joseph should be an encouragement to all men. When a man says "no" to the seductress with her longing eyes (see Proverbs 5:1–23) he will save his own soul from death and receive promotion from God in life.

> You have heard that it was said to those of old, "You shall not commit adultery." But I say to you that whoever looks at a woman to lust for her has already committed adultery with her in his heart.
> —MATTHEW 5:27–28

It is possible to commit adultery with someone without actually having sex with them. When you look at someone lustfully and desire to have sex with that person or have sexual fantasies about someone other than your husband or

80

The Seventh Commandment

wife, you have already committed adultery with that person in your heart.

Jesus warns against this type of lustful desire, the only way to resist this type of temptation is by self-denial and by being filled with the Spirit of God. Adultery breaks the bond of trust between married couples. Once this bond of trust is broken it can rarely be repaired. Adultery ultimately leads to divorce. Divorce divides the family unit and results in angry, unhappy and insecure children who eventually grow up to be angry adults in society who end up following the same example as their emotionally damaged parents. We are then left with an emotionally dysfunctional society. God never intended for a married couple to divorce, divorce upsets God's original created order that was established in the Garden of Eden between Adam and Eve, the order of marriage, a covenant relationship between a man and a woman for life.

Jesus says in Matthew 5:32, "But I say to you whoever divorces his wife for any reason except sexual immorality causes her to commit adultery; and whoever marries a woman who is divorced commits adultery."

In this scripture Jesus was addressing the Pharisees concerning marriage and divorce. The Pharisees interpreted Moses' Law, the Ten Commandments as saying that a man could divorce his wife for any reason he felt valid. Jesus explains to the Pharisees that divorce was only permitted on the grounds of sexual immorality such as homosexuality, adultery, fornication and prostitution.

This scripture still applies to Christian marriages today, unless one partner has been sexually unfaithful to the other, there is no valid reason for divorce. A Christian marriage should bear witness to the world that marriage is a covenant

81

DIVINE SPIRITUAL LAWS

relationship between a man and a woman and this relationship should blossom into a life together based on love, forgiveness and reconciliation under the Lordship of Christ.

> Likewise also the men, leaving the natural use of the woman, burning in their lust for one another, men with men committing what is shameful, and receiving in themselves the penalty of their error which was due.
> —ROMANS 1:27

A society that has reached such shamefully exposed levels of homosexuality is in total rebellion against God. We just have to watch the sitcoms that are spewed out in America season after season to see a nation in rebellion against God, not to mention the nations that purchase these ungodly sitcoms and view them on prime-time television. The rise of homosexuality in society is a sign that a society is in the last stages of decay. The Old Testament was very clear on the subject of homosexuality, "You shall not lie with a male as with a woman. It is an abomination" (Lev. 18:22).

All homosexual relationships were forbidden, whether it was a man lying with a man or a woman lying with a woman as with a man, it was an abomination before the eyes of the Lord and still is today. In the Old Testament those that practiced homosexuality were removed from the congregation of Israel and executed.

Genesis 19:12–29 is an example of God's judgment toward the sin of homosexuality, the Lord rained brimstone and fire on Sodom and Gomorrah and everyone perished except Lot and his family. When God made man, He made man in His image and He made man male and female (Gen. 1:27). When two men practice sodomy with one another, they are defiling the image of God and the natural order of creation and this

The Seventh Commandment

is an abomination before the Lord. Satan strives to defile the image of God and uses fallen man to achieve his purposes. A person is not born a homosexual, God made man either male or female. God does not make mistakes. Psalm 139:13 reads, "For You formed my inward parts; You covered me in my mother's womb."

The Lord knew us before we were born and formed our "inward parts" in our mother's womb. Today God still judges homosexuality as a sin. The Word of God says that the Lord will give these sinners over to a debased mind. Debased is to "lower the quality or character of," the homosexuals mind and reasoning and judgment becomes lowered as well as his/her character in society. That is why the homosexual constantly fights for society to accept and recognize their sinful behavior as normal because this type of behavior is not acceptable to God. They do not have the mind of Christ (Phil. 2:5). There is no sin that is too great or too small that God will not forgive. The Lord will hold back His judgment for a while to give the sinner the opportunity to repent, should a sinner refuse to repent when given ample opportunity, God will pass judgment upon the sinner (2 Pet. 3:9). The Lord will not lower His standards with regards to sin, He is Holy and He is God and He does not tolerate sin and disobedience toward His Word.

Chapter 11

THE EIGHTH COMMANDMENT

"You shall not steal."

—EXODUS 20:15

The earth is the Lord's, and all its fullness, the world and those who dwell therein.

—PSALM 24:1

DIVINE SPIRITUAL LAWS

EVERYTHING IN THIS world belongs to God, the earth, the animal life and humanity. God decides whom He will bless as Proverbs 10:22 tells us, "The blessing of the Lord makes one rich, and He adds no sorrow with it."

When someone steals something from another person, he has taken something without the owner's permission and has no intent of returning this item back to its rightful owner. When a thief steals from someone, he is actually stealing from God. In the Old Testament there were many laws set in place to discourage stealing. Israelites were not allowed to steal or cheat or rob a neighbor. (See Leviticus 19:11–13.) If a thief stole an ox or donkey or sheep and it was still alive, the thief would have to pay back double (Exod. 22:4). If someone kidnapped a man and sold him, the thief was put to death (Exod. 21:16). If a thief stole food, he had to restore back to the owner sevenfold (Prov. 6:30–31).

The Lord passes serious judgment upon the thief, "I will send out the curse," says the Lord of hosts; "It shall enter the house of the thief and the house of the one who swears falsely by My name. It shall remain in the midst of his house and consume it, with its timber and stones" (Zech. 5:4).

When someone steals from another person, whether it's an object, money, the company's time or petrol, they bring a curse upon themselves; this curse remains in the midst of the thief's house and consumes everything in his house and pertaining to his house. The thief will always be lacking,

86

The Eighth Commandment

lacking money, lacking food and lacking funds to repair his house, which will be consumed from the inside out. In John 10:10, Jesus gives the characteristics of a thief, "The thief does not come except to steal, and to kill, and to destroy. I have come that they may have life, and that they may have it more abundantly."

A thief is motivated by his covetous eye and evil nature, he is lazy and self-seeking and his father is the devil.

> Will a man rob God? Yet you have robbed Me! But you say, "In what way have we robbed You?" In tithes and offerings.
>
> —MALACHI 3:8

The topic of tithes and offerings is a touchy subject when it comes to Christians. A lot of churches are guilty of putting people in bondage pertaining to tithes and offerings. Unfortunately, we are guilty of robbing God when we do not tithe correctly. As Christians we are to tithe 10 percent of our full income after deductions. Your offering is separate to your tithe; the Holy Spirit will lay on your heart what amount your offering should be. If you are attending a local church, you give your tithe to that church. Wherever you are being spiritually fed, is where you should pay your tithe. There is a powerful promise to those who bring the tithe into the storehouse (church).

God says, "And try Me now in this, Says the Lord of hosts, 'If I will not open for you the window of heaven and pour out for you such blessing that there will not be room enough to receive it. And I will rebuke the devourer for your sakes, so that he will not destroy the fruit of your ground, not shall the vine fail to bear fruit for you in the field.'" (Mal. 3:10–11).

God Himself will open the window of heaven and bless

DIVINE SPIRITUAL LAWS

you more than you could have ever imagined. He will rebuke the devourer (Satan) from devouring your finances. We can never out- give God, He says in verse 10, "And try Me now in this," This is a challenge from God to us, give Him an opportunity to prove His faithfulness to you and bless you.

> And He said to them, "It is written, My house shall be called a house of prayer, but you have made it a den of thieves."
>
> —MATTHEW 21:13

Jesus overturned the tables of the moneychangers and of those who sold livestock in the temple because they were over charging foreigners who had come into Jerusalem to worship at the temple. These traders were performing transactions of theft in the house of God. The temple was a place of prayer and worship, not a place to legalize theft.

I would like to share my personal testimony with regards to this commandment on stealing. I live in a country where stealing is a booming business amongst the unemployed, unfortunately these thieves are violent and abusive and murder innocent citizens daily over menial possessions such as a cell phone, a vehicle or a handbag. My testimony is based on a scripture the Lord gave to me during this difficult time in my life, Hebrews 11:6, "But without faith it is impossible to please Him, for he who comes to God must believe that He is, and that He is a rewarder of those who diligently seek Him."

In the beginning of 2009 I went through a traumatic experience in my life where God allowed my character to be attacked by Satan himself. It was the beginning of a new year and I had just completed a seven day fast. The fast had been quite a challenge both physically and spiritually for me. The Lord had set me free during this fast from many childhood

88

The Eighth Commandment

hurts and demonic strongholds that had been over my life since my troubled childhood. This attack from Satan took me by total surprise. I was unaware at the time of the powerful spiritual implications of fasting, that when we fast and pray the enemy comes in with all his power to tempt and attack us.

> And when He (Jesus) had fasted forty days and forty nights, afterward He was hungry. Now when the tempter (Satan) came to Him, he said, "If you are the Son of God, command that these stones become bread."
> —MATTHEW 4:2

When we fast and pray we cause havoc in the spiritual realm, Satan hates a fasting Christian and will do anything in his power to discourage and prevent Christian's from fasting on a regular basis. I decided to diligently seek the Lord for an answer to why this attack had happened in my life. I sought the Lord for six weeks day and night after this demonic attack in which my life had been threatened at gun point in my own home by three aggressive criminals who assaulted me and then proceeded to steal all of our household valuables.

The Lord led me to Job 1:6–12, where Satan attacks Job's character. Satan comes before the presence of the Lord with a host of celestial beings.

God asks Satan, "From where do you come?" Satan replies, "From going to and fro on the earth, and from walking back and forth on it."

Once a year, all the celestial beings are summoned by God to come into His presence and give an account for their actions over the past year. Celestial beings are accountable to

89

DIVINE SPIRITUAL LAWS

God; even Satan is accountable to God. Satan can do nothing on this earth without God's permission.

Then the Lord says to Satan, "Have you considered My servant Job, that there is none like him on the earth, a blameless and upright man, one who fears God and shuns evil?" Satan replies, "Does Job fear God for nothing? Have you not made a hedge around him, around his household, and around all that he has on every side?"

Further on in Job 1:12, God gives Satan power over all that Job has but Satan is not to lay a hand on Job's person. Satan does not have the authority or permission from God to take Job's life.

This is when I realized that God had given Satan permission to come into my home and take what he wanted and terrorize and threaten my life but Satan was not given permission to kill me. God had for just a moment removed His hedge of protection from around me and my home and allowed the enemy in. Job's life is evidence and a record of how God can work in a believer's life. As Christian's we often blame the devil when a situation looks bleak in our lives or tribulation comes our way, when it is actually the work of the Lord (Rev. 2:10). When we encounter situations like this in our lives, this is when we need the spirit of discernment.

Discernment is to be able to spiritually discern between an attack from the enemy because of sin in our lives or the Lord allowing the enemy to enter in to test our character and faith in God. Another confirmation that this was a test from God in my life was that I had just turned forty. In biblical numerics the number forty represents "trials and testing." Nevertheless, I chose to believe God's Word and trust in Him no matter how alone and fearful I felt at times. Fear is the opposite of faith, to live in fear is a lack of faith in God.

90

The Eighth Commandment

For God has not given us a spirit of fear, but of power
and of love and of a sound mind.

—2 TIMOTHY 1:7

Faith grows in our hearts when we hear God's Word, "So
then faith comes by hearing, and hearing by the Word of
God" (Rom. 10:17).

When we live in fear we have no faith in God and we don't
believe His Word. By meditating on the Word of God daily
our faith is strengthened and our hope is restored. Nine
months after this attack on my life and not giving in to the
flooding emotions of fear, hopelessness and doubt, the Lord
rewarded me openly for diligently seeking Him through this
trial and for not wavering in my faith. God is a God of restoration, everything that Job originally lost was restored to
him double in his latter days. (Job 42:12–13) In October 2009,
Hebrews 11:6 became a reality in my life. The Lord blessed me
miraculously with a property to the value of 1.8 million Rand
(approximately $228,000). God rewards us here on earth not
only in heaven when we overcome trials in our walk with
Him. After this attack on my life I could have chosen to turn
away from God and not trust Him, but I chose to seek Him
and continued to serve Him faithfully and He rewarded my
faith publicly. God is faithful and His Word is true, some-
times these blessings come at a price, the price of a trial
through which God can miraculously bless you depending
on your attitude and faith in Him.

Chapter 12

THE NINTH COMMANDMENT

"You shall not bear false witness against your neighbor."

—EXODUS 20:16

DIVINE SPIRITUAL LAWS

THE NINTH COMMANDMENT called the Israelites to be trustworthy and truthful in all their dealings with one another. They were to refrain from lying to one another, slandering one another or bearing false witness against one another. The Israelites were to take on the nature of their God.

> God is not a man, that He should lie, nor a son of man, that He should repent.
>
> —NUMBERS 23:19

God cannot lie; lying is not in His character, "In hope of eternal life which God, who cannot lie, promised before time began" (Titus 1:2).

When someone continually lies, they are submitting to the father of all lies, Satan. Jesus says in John 8:44 when confronting the Jewish people, "You are of your father the devil, and the desires of your father you want to do. He was a murderer from the beginning, and does not stand in the truth, because there is no truth in him. When he speaks a lie, he speaks from his own resources, for he is a liar and the father of it."

To accuse God of any wrong doing is as the sin of blasphemy. Satan is the accuser of the brethren, he accuses the brethren before our God, day and night, "Then I heard a loud voice saying in heaven, "Now salvation, and strength, and the kingdom of our God, and the power of His Christ have come,

The Ninth Commandment

for the accuser of our brethren, who accused them before our God day and night; has been cast down" (Rev. 12:10).

To slander and lie and accuse someone falsely is a sure indication that a person is motivated by Satan and he is their father.

> "But a certain man named Ananias, with Sapphira his wife, sold a possession. And kept back part of the proceeds, his wife also being aware of it, and brought a certain part and laid it at the apostle's feet. But Peter said, 'Ananias, why has Satan filled your heart to lie to the Holy Spirit and keep back part of the price of the land for yourself? While it remained, was it not your own? And after it was sold, was it not in your own control? Why have you conceived this thing in your heart? You have not lied to men but to God.' Then Ananias, hearing these words, fell down and breathed his last. So great fear came upon all those who heard these things."
>
> —ACTS 5:1–5

Ananias and Sapphira were judged by God for their hypocrisy as members of the church and for lying to the Holy Spirit, not for their decision to keep a part of the proceeds from the property that they had sold for themselves.

Three hours after the death of her husband, Sapphira comes before Peter not knowing what has just happened to her husband and lies to Peter and the Holy Spirit concerning the price of the property they had sold. She falls down immediately at Peter's feet and breathes her last breath. This is a severe judgment upon the lives of Ananias and Sapphira. They were members of the early church and this severe judgment upon them displays God's standard with regards to lying and hypocrisy in the church.

DIVINE SPIRITUAL LAWS

As disciples of Christ, we need to meditate daily on the Word of God and be led by the Holy Spirit in order to have the strength and power to reject the temptations from the enemy. As disciples of Christ we are also to set a godly example of how a Christian should act and behave in society, our holy lifestyle should encourage the unsaved to join their local church. Many saved and unsaved people end up turning away from the church and ultimately God because of the hypocritical lifestyle of church members and church leaders.

> Beware of false prophets, who come to you in sheep's clothing, but inwardly they are ravenous wolves. You will know them by their fruits. Do men gather grapes from thorn bushes or figs from thistles? Even so, every good tree bears good fruit, but a bad tree bears bad fruit. A good tree cannot bear bad fruit, nor can a bad tree bear good fruit. Every tree that does not bear good fruit is cut down and thrown into the fire. Therefore by their fruits you will know them.
> —MATTHEW 7:15–20

A false prophet is someone who speaks lies and artificial truths about the things of God. Many false prophets come in sheep's clothing pretending to be Christian guides. These false prophets disguise themselves as pastors, members of the congregation, elders and even deacons. Unfortunately their real motives are self-centeredness, control, manipulation and division. Every Christian needs to test a false or lying prophet by their fruit, their fruit is their lifestyle, are they living a life-style according to the standard of the Bible? Another fruit is their character, are they holy, loyal, reliable and truthful? What do they teach? Do they teach the truth about the Word of God or half-truths and lies? The Lord

96

The Ninth Commandment

says that every tree that does not bear "good fruit" will be cut down and thrown into the fire, the Lord will pass His judgment upon the false and lying prophet who manipulates the Word of God with false teachings to bring division and destruction in the body of Christ.

> And the tongue is a fire, a world of iniquity. The tongue is so set among our members that it defiles the whole body, and sets on fire the course of nature; and it is set on fire by hell.
>
> —JAMES 3:6

The words we speak will either give life or bring death into a situation. When the Lord created the heavens and the earth, He spoke them into existence, imagine how much creative power was released when God said, "Let there be light." As Christians, the words we speak bear the same authority today. When we are saved and born-again our dominion over creation has now been restored through the death of Christ on the cross. The words we speak over one another can either bring life into a situation or bring death and destruction. The tongue is referred to as a fire, think of how quickly a fire spreads once it has started. When a rumor is spread about a fellow brethren it spreads like a wild fire and its origin is from hell.

We need to constantly keep our tongue tamed. It can become a weapon for the enemy to use at his will if we do not keep it under control.

> Speaking to one another in psalms and hymns and spiritual songs, singing and making melody in your heart to the Lord.
>
> —EPHESIANS 5:19

DIVINE SPIRITUAL LAWS

We need to be continually filled with the Holy Spirit, speaking to one another in psalms, hymns and spiritual songs. When we are making melody in our hearts to the Lord, there will be no room for slander or gossip or lying, only place for praise and thanksgiving unto the Lord.

Chapter 13

THE TENTH COMMANDMENT

"You shall not covet."

—Exodus 20:17

DIVINE SPIRITUAL LAWS

To COVET IS to desire or lust after something that belongs to someone else. Wanting something is not a sin, but when this wanting is motivated by envy or jealousy, then it becomes coveting. The Israelites where forbidden to covet a neighbor's wife, his male or female servant, nor his ox, nor his donkey or anything that belonged to his neighbor. They were not to covet the enemy's treasures or belongings after they had won a battle, as the enemy's belongings were considered 'accursed things,' only with God's permission where the Israelites permitted to collect the spoils after a victory over a enemy in battle.

> And Achan answered Joshua and said, "Indeed I have sinned against the Lord God of Israel, and this is what I have done: When I saw among the spoils a beautiful Babylonian garment, two hundred shekels of silver, and a wedge of gold weighing fifty shekels, I coveted them and took them. And there they are, hidden in the earth in the midst of my tent, with the silver under it."
> —JOSHUA 7:20–21

The Israelites were fighting a battle against the Amorites at Ai and were being defeated. The main cause of their defeat against the Amorites, (who had the smaller army) was due to the fact that Achan had taken and coveted the 'accursed things' from the battle of Jericho. The Lord had given clear instructions to Joshua that the Israelites were not to bring any 'accursed things' that belonged to the inhabitants of Jericho

The Tenth Commandment

into the Israelites camp. These 'accursed things' would make the camp of Israel a curse and trouble it. Accursed means, under a curse, often these 'accursed things' were idols or items of clothing and treasures that were used in idol worship by these pagan tribes. The Israelites were forbidden from coveting the enemies' riches and possessions, they were not to covet the world's possessions, God was their treasure and He would provide for them in every way. Because Achan had taken these 'accursed things' he had brought a curse on the whole nation of Israel and not just upon himself.

> Then Joshua, and all Israel with him, took Achan the son of Zerah, the silver, the garment, the wedge of gold, his sons, his daughters, his oxen, his donkeys, his sheep, his tent, and all that he had, and they brought them to the Valley of Achor. And Joshua said, 'Why have you troubled us? The Lord will trouble you this day.' So all Israel stoned him with stones; and they burned them with fire after they had stoned them with stones.
>
> —Joshua 7:24–25

Achan and his family as well as his tent his livestock and the 'accursed things' were all destroyed, the Lord made an example of Achan, Israel was to obey God. After this incident, Israel went on to defeat the Amorites at Ai and the Lord permitted them to take the spoils at Ai as a reward for their obedience to God. When we steal or covet our neighbors' belongings we bring a curse upon our lives as well as the lives of our sons, daughters, our home and everything we own. Achan was responsible for the loss of his life, his sons lives, his daughters' lives, the live-stock and his home were all destroyed by fire, because of his disobedience toward God's commandment.

101

DIVINE SPIRITUAL LAWS

> And He (Jesus) said to them, "Take heed and beware
> of covetousness, for one's life does not consist in the
> abundance of the things he possesses."
>
> —LUKE 12:15

Jesus was using this parable of the rich fool to drive home
the true meaning of "life." Life in Christ has nothing to do
with acquiring possessions here on earth. After all, we cannot
take these possessions, which we accumulate here on earth
with us when we die. Possessions do not give life or provide
permanent security because death ultimately separates us
from them. Our riches and treasures should lie within our
hearts, in our relationship with Christ.

> Jesus says, "But seek first the kingdom of God and His
> righteousness, and all these things shall be added to
> you."
>
> —MATTHEW 6:33

When we seek "first" the kingdom of God and His righteousness, then God will add all these things unto us. God
has pledged Himself through His covenant faithfulness to
respond to our needs (not our greed) when we seek Him
"first" above all else.

> Let your conduct be without covetousness; be content
> with such things as you have. For He Himself has said,
> "I will never leave you nor forsake you."
>
> —HEBREWS 13:5

Covetousness and financial fear can be overcome when we
have a spiritual relationship with God our Father. God said,
"I will never leave you nor forsake you."

When we are content with our partner, our children our

102

The Tenth Commandment

homes or the vehicle we drive, we will not desire anything God has not already given us. In a world where the financial market is so vulnerable and unpredictable, Christian's need to be firmly rooted in the Word of God and believe in God's covenant promise of provision toward those who love and obey Him.

> Therefore I say to you, do not worry about your life, what you will eat or what you will drink; nor about your body, what you will put on. Is not life more than food and the body more than clothing?
>
> —MATTHEW 6:25

Jesus says in this scripture that a Christian has no need to worry (stress, anxiety and pressure) about his daily needs being met. To worry is unnecessary and unfruitful in a Christian's life. A Christian lives by faith and faith in God produces fruit in a Christian's life.

> Now faith is the substance of things hoped for, the evidence of things not seen.
>
> —HEBREWS 11:1

The Greek word translated "substance" means "a standing under" and is used in the sense of a "title deed." A title deed is a legal document giving evidence of a person's right to own a property. Therefore, faith is the "title deed" of things hoped for. When we stand under faith we are standing on the promises of God over our lives. When we exercise our faith in God, He is faithful and true to His word and will reward our faith in Him with all the things we ever hoped for and could never have imagined seeing or receiving, this type of faith in God provides us with our heart's desire (Ps. 20:4).

103

Chapter 14

THE BRIDE OF CHRIST

Take heed that no one deceives you. For many will come in My name, saying, 'I am the Christ,' and will deceive many. And you will hear of wars and rumors of wars. See that you are not troubled; for all these things must come to pass, but the end in not yet. For nation will rise against nation, and kingdom against kingdom. And there will be famines, pestilences, and earthquakes in various places. All these are the beginning of sorrows. Then they will deliver you up to tribulation and kill you, and you will be hated by all nations for My name's sake. And then many will be offended, will betray one another, and will hate one another. Then many false prophets will rise up and deceive many. And because lawlessness will abound, the love of many will grow cold. But he who endures to the end shall be saved. And this gospel of the kingdom will be preached in all the world as a witness to all the nations, and then the end will come.

—MATTHEW 24:4–14

DIVINE SPIRITUAL LAWS

THIS AGE WE are living in (the age of fallen man) will eventually come to an end. In Matthew 24:4, Jesus was teaching His disciples in private on the Mount of Olives. He taught that at the end of the Age there will be religious deception, social and political unrest, natural disasters, disloyalty and persecution of Christians. All these signs will precede the end times. Even in the midst of all these difficulties the followers of Christ are to persevere in spreading the gospel of the kingdom to all the world and are encouraged to endure to the end.

The beginning of sorrows are the "labor pains" this age will experience before the birth of the age to come. The age to come is the age where Jesus will rule and reign as King over all the earth.

> Repent therefore and be converted, that your sins may be blotted out, so that times of refreshing may come from the presence of the Lord, and that He may send Jesus Christ, who was preached to you before, whom heaven must receive until times of restoration of all things, which God has spoken by the mouth of all His holy prophets since the world began.
>
> —ACTS 3:19–21

The bride of Christ (the church) needs to make herself ready for the return of the Bridegroom (Rev. 19:6–8). The Bridegroom, who is Jesus, will not be returning for a defiled and defeated bride. The church therefore needs to come to

The Bride of Christ

a place of repentance and be converted to Christ, so that her sins may be blotted out. Proper Christian behavior will hasten the coming of the Day of the Lord. (2 Peter 3:12)

> ...that He might present her to Himself a glorious church, not having spot or wrinkle or any such thing, but that she should be holy and without blemish.
>
> —EPHESIANS 5:27

Jesus is returning for a holy, glorious bride without the blemish of sin. The glorious bride will be adorned with the gifts God has given her, the gifts of the Spirit. These gifts are the word of wisdom, the word of knowledge, faith, gifts of healing, working of miracles, prophecy, discerning of spirits, different kinds of tongues and the interpretation of tongues. The church will be operating in all nine of these gifts of the Spirit.

Once the bride's sins have been blotted out, times of refreshing will come from the presence of the Lord, the Holy Spirit will cleanse, anoint and equip the church for her purpose of spreading the end time gospel of Jesus Christ. The glorious bride of Christ will be functioning fully in all of the nine gifts of the Spirit. Heaven must receive Jesus until the times of restoration of all things, this is when each and every person has had the opportunity to repent and be restored to God through Jesus Christ, only then will Jesus return for His bride and together they will rule and reign upon the earth. The ultimate restoration is the return of the church, Christ's bride in all her majesty and glory as God intended her to be. Jesus is currently sharing His Father's throne in heaven, Jesus is waiting to establish His kingdom here on earth with His beloved Bride, the church. Jesus' return is based on the sanctification of His Bride. The church needs to go back to

DIVINE SPIRITUAL LAWS

the basics of Christianity. The birth of the early church came
after the death of Christ. A church operating without the
direction of the Holy Spirit and without Christ as its Head is
a dead church that has no access to God the Father.

As long as the church remains in its current state of leth-
argy toward the commandments of God and His word, the
"times of refreshing" will be held back. The Lord will not
force His will upon humanity. Man has to choose to serve
God out of his love for God. When the bride is ready and
holy and sanctified, Jesus will return for her in all His glory.
What are we waiting for? As Christians we need to arise and
shine and fulfill our destiny as the bride of Christ.

> All authority has been given to Me in heaven and
> on earth. Go therefore and make disciples of all the
> nations, baptizing them in the name of the Father and
> of the Son and of the Holy Spirit, teaching them to
> observe all things that I have commanded you; and lo,
> I am with you always, even to the end of the age. Amen.
> —MATTHEW 28:18–20

The great commission of the church is to make disciples of
all the nations. Churches today are more concerned about how
many members they have warming their pews each and every
Sunday instead of focusing on how many members are being
discipled correctly according to the Word of God. Church is
not a place to be entertained by glory seeking preachers or a
place to have your ears tickled by false teachings that make
you "feel" good and never address the seriousness of sin and
the value of repentance before God. Unfortunately the "world"
and the ways of this "world" have entered the church today,
false teachings are accepted and preached in most churches
today, messages of universalism and postmodern theology.
The only message that should be preached and taught in

108

The Bride of Christ

our churches is the salvation message of Jesus Christ. Only through Christ can we be saved and set free and reconciled to God. The End-Time church of Christ will be baptizing disciples of Christ in the name of the Father and of the Son and of the Holy Spirit, which means these disciples of Christ will be filled with the Holy Spirit they will speak in tongues and operate in the gifts of the Spirit. These disciples of Jesus Christ will spread the gospel of Christ, heal the sick, raise the dead and perform signs and wonders in the name of Jesus.

In John 14:12, Jesus says, "Most assuredly, I say to you, he who believes in Me, the works that I do he will do also; and greater works than these he will do, because I go to My Father."

The church of Christ is commissioned to reach a "greater" number of unsaved people through the preaching of the gospel of Christ. The end-time church will be a glorious church obeying God's word and His commandments. The end-time church will not be a church plagued by sexual scandals or be ashamed of her leadership practicing divorce and adultery on a regular basis causing the whole body of Christ to be defiled, divided and led astray without a true shepherd. In 2 Peter 2:1–2, Peter warns against false teachers that will characterize the "church age" and these false teachings will increase "in the latter times." These false teachers have already infiltrated our churches today, they are recognizable by their fruits/character, these false teachers display carnal character traits such as sensuality they are arrogant, self-indulgent and self-seeking with little or no conscience toward the moral teachings or biblical standards written in the Word of God.

Jesus said that all authority has been given to Him in heaven and on earth, when we are born again we become kings and priests in the kingdom of God, we now have the

DIVINE SPIRITUAL LAWS

same authority over heaven and earth because of the death of Jesus on the cross.

> ...and has made us kings and priests to His God and Father, to Him be glory and dominion forever and ever. Amen.
>
> —REVELATION 1:6

The End-Time church will be holy and sanctified unto the Lord; she will be full of the glory and power of Christ and a glorious example to the unsaved in the world. When this current "age" comes to an end, which is the "age of fallen man," a new "age" will begin with Jesus Christ as Lord and King!

> And it shall come to pass in the last days, says God, that I will pour out of My Spirit on all flesh; your sons and your daughters shall prophesy, your young men shall see visions, your old men shall dream dreams. And on My menservants and on My maidservants I will pour out My Spirit in those days; and they shall prophesy. I will show wonders in heaven above and signs in the earth beneath; blood and fire and vapor of smoke. The sun shall be turned into darkness, and the moon into blood, before the coming of the great and awesome day of the Lord. And it shall come to pass that whoever calls on the name of the Lord shall be saved.
>
> —ACTS 2:17–21

The "last days" refers to the time from the birth of the early church at Pentecost to the return of Christ. The outpouring of the Holy Spirit in the "last days" will be on all flesh, not just an outpouring upon those in the upper room as on the day of Pentecost. Whether you are a servant or a successful businessman, if you believe in Jesus the latter outpouring of

110

The Bride of Christ

the Holy Spirit will be greater than the former outpouring of the Holy Spirit at Pentecost. This outpouring of the Holy Spirit can only come once the church has reached a place of repentance, we are currently living in the last days, the past two thousand years have been the last days. The heavens and the earth will display wonders preceding the great and awesome day of the Lord, whoever calls on the name of the Lord during that time will be saved. Who is the church? We are the church, if you are a born- again Christian, you are the temple of God. When Christian's unite and assemble together in fellowship in the name of Jesus Christ, they are the bride of Christ.

> A new commandment I give to you, that you love one another; as I have loved you, that you also love one another. By this all will know that you are My disciples, if you have love for one another.
>
> —JOHN 13:34–35

This "love" Jesus is speaking about is a new standard of "love." It is the "love" of Jesus. A true disciple of Christ has a servant's heart and a selfless love toward others. When a disciple displays this type of love toward humanity they are a true witness of Christ to the unsaved in the world. Jesus has set a new standard of love for humanity to follow.

He has raised the bar when it comes to love. As the bride of Christ we need to raise the standard of love in our marriages, work place, families, communities, churches and nation, we need to be true disciples of Christ, a role model for those who are lost without Christ in the world. In Matthew 24:12, Jesus teaches that because lawlessness will abound at the end of this Age, the love of many will grow cold. The world needs to believe and see that God is alive and His word is true, the

DIVINE SPIRITUAL LAWS

world sees Christ through the church; the church needs to raise its standard of love and holiness to the standard of God's word, this means no more compromising.

> Then He (Jesus) said to His disciples, "The harvest truly is plentiful, but the laborers are few. Therefore pray the Lord of the harvest to send out laborers into His harvest."
>
> —MATTHEW 9:37–38

The "harvest" is those believers that are weary and scattered like sheep having no shepherd. The harvest is "His" harvest, these people belong to God. Jesus commissions us to pray to the Lord for laborers for the harvest. Spirit filled leaders (laborers) need to be raised up by God through our prayers to bring this harvest into the kingdom of God. This is why Jesus died on the cross, to save man from eternal damnation because of sin and to reconcile man to God. There is no other mediator between man and God, only Jesus. This is the commission of the bride of Christ before her Groom returns.

> Arise, shine; for your light has come! And the glory of the Lord is risen upon you. For behold, the darkness shall cover the earth, and deep darkness the people; but the Lord will arise over you, and His glory will be seen upon you. The Gentiles shall come to your light, and kings to the brightness of your rising.
>
> —ISAIAH 60:1–3

Isaiah 60 calls the church to "arise" and "shine." The church needs to arise, wake- up out of its slumber and start to shine forth in righteousness for Jesus Christ. The "glory" of the Lord, represents honor, splendor, power, wealth, and

The Bride of Christ

authority, which God is waiting to impart upon the church once she has risen to the standard of God's word. In the last days great darkness will cover the earth and "deep" darkness the people, we have established that we are already living in the "last days" and the evil intentions of men's hearts are increasing daily. The bride of Christ needs to arise and shine with the glory of the Lord, then the unsaved will be drawn to her light and the nations (leaders) will seek her for Godly direction and counsel. The church leaders, who are the pastors, deacons and elders need to "arise and shine" out of their comfort zones and begin to fast and pray and seek the Lord's direction and purpose with regards to their congregations, families and their nations.

Second Chronicles 7:14 says, "If My people (the Christian's) who are called by My name will humble (fast) themselves, and pray and seek My face, and turn (repent) from their wicked ways, then I will hear from heaven, and will forgive their sin and heal their land."

No matter what country you live in around the world, we all need God to hear our prayers in heaven, we all need forgiveness of our sins and we all need our land (nation) healed. Every nation around the world today is in desperate need of a Savior. The world is in a state of financial chaos, moral degradation and increasing in lawlessness, there is only one Leader (King) who can redeem and save fallen man, this King is Jesus.

The day of the Lord will come as a thief in the night, in which the heavens will pass away with a great noise, and the elements will melt with fervent heat; both the earth and the works that are in it will be burnt up. Therefore, since all these things will be dissolved, what manner of persons ought you to be in holy conduct and godliness, looking for and

DIVINE SPIRITUAL LAWS

hastening the coming of the day of God, because of which the heavens will be dissolved, being on fire, and the elements will melt with fervent heat? Nevertheless we, according to His promise, look for new heavens and a new earth in which righteousness dwells (2 Pet. 3:10–13).

Proper righteous Christian behavior will hasten the coming of the day of the Lord Jesus. The timing of the Lord's return is directly related to the condition and righteous behavior of the church. The Lord's return will be sudden and unexpected, as believers of Christ we are to still look for His promise despite what the scoffers say concerning the coming of the day of the Lord. Our promise as followers of Christ is the promise of His return and the promise of a new heaven and a new earth in which righteousness dwells. This passage of scripture is a warning to the body of Christ, we should be living a holy, God centered life, any other lifestyle will be destroyed when the Lord returns, both the earth and the works (man and his works) that are in it will be burnt up and the heavens will pass away with a great noise! What manner of persons ought we to be?

> Then Simon Peter came, following him, and went into the tomb; and he saw the linen cloths lying there, and the handkerchief that had been around His head, not lying with the linen cloths, but folded together in a place by itself.
>
> —JOHN 20:6–7

The grave-clothes with which Jesus' body had been wrapped in were not unwound or disarranged when Simon Peter entered the tomb. The grave-clothes still retained the shape of Jesus' body, only the upper layer had fallen down

The Bride of Christ

upon the lower layer and the head wrapping (handkerchief) had been removed by Jesus and folded and placed by itself.

Jesus' body had passed through the burial shroud, He had not unwrapped Himself when He rose from the dead, He passed right through the linen cloths. There is significance to the fact that His head wrapping was folded and placed separately by itself. According to Jewish custom in those days, when the master of the house was dining at his table and he left the table and was not going to return he would leave his handkerchief unfolded on the table as an indication to his servants that they could tidy and clear the table. If the master left the table and was to return he would fold his handkerchief and set it aside as an indication to his servants that he would be returning. Jesus left all of humanity a message, a sign in the tomb when He rose from the dead, He is coming back!

If you are not born again and would like to meet with Jesus, pray this prayer out aloud to the Lord:

> *Father God, I ask you to forgive me of all my sins. Lord I believe that Jesus is Your Son and that He died on the cross and rose from the dead. Lord Jesus, I ask You to come into my life and save me, heal me and deliver me from all temptation . . . In Jesus name I pray, amen.*

Romans 10:9–10 informs us, "…if you confess with your mouth the Lord Jesus and believe in your heart that God has raised Him from the dead, you will be saved. For with the heart one believes unto righteousness, and with the mouth confession is made unto salvation."

DIVINE SPIRITUAL LAWS

> Most assuredly, I say to you, unless one is born again,
> he cannot see the kingdom of God.
>
> —JOHN 3:3

Being born again is not a second biological birth here on earth; it is a spiritual birth from God above when you receive Jesus Christ as your Lord and Savior. Amen.

ABOUT THE AUTHOR

CHANTAL R. NIELSEN is a wife and mother of three beautiful children and resides in Johannesburg, South Africa. She gave her life to the Lord at the age of twelve and has been a maidservant of the Lord serving in ministry over the years as a worship leader and songwriter. Two years ago the Lord gave her the title for "Divine Spiritual Laws" and she began the journey of writing her first book out of obedience to the Lord. This book was completed while she was on a forty-day fast, seeking God's direction and guidance for her family's life as well as seeking out the true plan and purpose for God's chosen people, the church— the bride of Christ.

CONTACT THE AUTHOR

WWW.CHANTALRNIELSEN.CO.ZA